C000001136

Business Coaching

BUSINESS COACHING

Achieving Practical Results
Through Effective Engagement

Peter Shaw and Robin Linnecar

CAPSTONE

Copyright © Peter Shaw and Robin Linnecar 2007

First published 2007
Capstone Publishing Ltd. (a Wiley Company)
The Atrium, Southern Gate, Chichester, PO19 8SQ, UK.
www.wileyeurope.com
Email (for orders and customer service enquires): cs-books@wiley.co.uk

The right of Peter Shaw and Robin Linnecar to be identified as the authors of this book has been asserted in accordance with the Copyright, Designs and Patents Act 1988

All Rights Reserved. No part of this publication may be reproduced, stored in a retrieval system or transmitted in any form or by any means, electronic, mechanical, photocopying, recording, scanning or otherwise, except under the terms of the Copyright, Designs and Patents Act 1988 or under the terms of a licence issued by the Copyright Licensing Agency Ltd, 90 Tottenham Court Road, London W1T 4LP, UK, without the permission in writing of the Publisher. Requests to the Publisher should be addressed to the Permissions Department, John Wiley & Sons Ltd, The Atrium, Southern Gate, Chichester, West Sussex PO19 8SQ, England, or emailed to permreq@wiley.co.uk, or faxed to (+44) 1243 770571.

Designations used by companies to distinguish their products are often claimed as trademarks. All brand names and product names used in this book are trade names, service marks, trademarks or registered trademarks of their respective owners. The Publisher is not associated with any product or vendor mentioned in this book. This publication is designed to provide accurate and authoritative information in regard to the subject matter covered. It is sold on the understanding that the Publisher is not engaged in rendering professional services. If professional advice or other expert assistance is required, the services of a competent professional should be sought.

Other Wiley Editorial Offices
John Wiley & Sons Inc., 111 River Street, Hoboken, NJ 07030, USA
Jossey-Bass, 989 Market Street, San Francisco, CA 94103–1741, USA
Wiley-VCH Verlag GmbH, Boschstr. 12, D-69469 Weinheim, Germany
John Wiley & Sons Australia Ltd, 42 McDougall Street, Milton, Queensland 4064, Australia
John Wiley & Sons (Asia) Pte Ltd, 2 Clementi Loop #02–01, Jin Xing Distripark, Singapore 129809
John Wiley & Sons Canada Ltd, 22 Worcester Road, Etobicoke, Ontario, Canada M9W 1L1
Wiley also publishes its books in a variety of electronic formats. Some content that appears in print may not be available in electronic books.

ISBN 978-1-84112-741-5

Library of Congress Cataloging-in-Publication Data
Shaw, Peter, CB.
 Business coaching : achieving practical results through effective engagement / Peter Shaw and Robin Linnecar.
   p. cm.
 Includes bibliographical references and index.
 ISBN 978-1-84112-741-5 (pbk. : alk. paper)
 1. Executive coaching. 2. Executives--Training of. 3. Leadership--Study and teaching. 4. Management--Study and teaching. 5. Executive ability. I. Linnecar, Robin. II. Title.
 HD30.4.S48 2007
 658.4'07124--dc22

                                                                      2007012098

Anniversary Logo Design: Richard J. Pacifico

Set in Photina by Sparks, Oxford – www.sparks.co.uk
Printed and bound in Great Britain by TJ International Ltd, Padstow, Cornwall

This book is printed on acid-free paper responsibly manufactured from sustainable forestry in which at least two trees are planted for each one used for paper production. Substantial discounts on bulk quantities of Capstone Books are available to corporations, professional associations and other organizations. For details telephone John Wiley & Sons on (+44) 1243–770441, fax (+44) 1243 770571 or email corporatedevelopment@wiley.co.uk

We dedicate this book to our families who are such an inspiration and continue to teach us what effective engagement means.

Contents

Acknowledgements

In writing a book about business coaching, it is impossible to acknowledge by name the many varied people, books and influences upon us, but there are certain groups of people who have been particularly influential.

We owe a great deal to our clients. We enjoy their company and the engagement with them over many different challenges. We have been on many varying journeys with clients: they have given us a richness of experience and understanding which we hope flows through this book.

We have benefited considerably from the wisdom of those who have extensive experience of investing in coaching. In particular we would like to thank Philippa Charles, Noel Hadden, Rob Edwards, Hilary Douglas, Jim McCaffery, Jill King and John Bailey for their practical insights. They represent a range of different worlds in the public and private sectors, but they share strong common feelings about professionalism, rigour and a focus on outcomes.

Many individuals gave extensively of their own personal experience as we prepared different chapters, especially Nick Brown, Phil Hodkinson, David Oliver and Jon Little. Judith Simpson and Nick Blandford were particularly helpful in working through examples of coaching programmes.

To our colleagues at Praesta Partners and Praesta International we owe an enormous debt of gratitude. The atmosphere of sharing and openness which Praesta possesses means that learning is not only pervasive, but is a delight. All our colleagues have been an invaluable source of ideas and encouragement, and many have helped us to sharpen the content, especially Mairi Eastwood, our Managing Partner, and Barry Woledge, our Chair. We take full responsibility for the ideas in the book while benefiting from the perspective of colleagues.

Our international colleague, Ron Hyams, has contributed some fascinating examples from South Africa in the international chapter, and Jane Upton has drawn on her insights from working as a coach in Spain.

We are indebted to Richard Donkin for his thoughtful foreword. Through the insightful writing in his column in the *Financial Times* and his books, Richard makes a major contribution to thinking through the impact of management change.

Sally Smith, who commissioned the book, has always been encouraging. John Moseley has been a thorough editor giving sound advice.

We owe a particular debt to Claire Pratt and Charlotte Gaudiano who have managed our diaries, enabling us to both see clients and to take forward this writing. Judy Smith has cheerfully borne the brunt of the typing work with valuable help from Ann Collins.

We want to thank our families, who have been so accepting of our disappearing into our respective studies to put finger to keyboard, pen to paper or mouth to Dictaphone. We are grateful for their long-suffering willingness to allow us to crystallize our thoughts in this book.

For Robin, special influences have been the teachers and professionals who coached him in rugby, hockey and cricket at school, university and beyond and the many business leaders for whom and with whom he has worked. His father's uprightness, wisdom and decisiveness and his mother's limitless listening ability were and are a beacon and benchmark in his life. Robin's wife, Joanna, has given him endless support and has kept his feet on the ground at all times. Staying engaged with their grown-up children, Rebecca, Ruth and Matthew, has shown what keeping in touch is all about.

For Peter, key influences have been the memory of his father's good sense, the practical wisdom of his mother, the level-headed advice of Frances, his spouse, and the insightfulness of their three children, Graham, Ruth and Colin. Those to whom he is particularly grateful for enabling him to develop coaching understanding include Jim Houston, David Normington, Rod Chamberlain and Bob Goodall.

An important context for us is the words from Proverbs Chapter 3: 'Blessed are those who find wisdom, those who gain understanding. For she is more profitable than silver and yields better results than gold.' We continue to search the depth of that wisdom. For us both personally, Jesus, in the way he listened to, challenged and coached people, has been an inspiration as a leader and we thank those of humility, stature and grace who introduced us to that person.

Finally, we want to acknowledge the support we have received from each other. Our backgrounds and temperaments are very different – that is why we choose to work together. Our journey through this book has been fun. We hope that it reads seamlessly, with two heads better than one!

Other books by Peter Shaw

Mirroring Jesus as Leader, Grove, 2004

Conversation Matters: How To Engage Effectively with One Another, Continuum, 2005

The Four Vs of Leadership: Vision, Values, Value-Added, Vitality, Capstone, 2006

Finding Your Future: The Second Time Around, Darton, Longman and Todd, 2006

Forthcoming Book

Making Difficult Decisions, Capstone, 2008

Foreword

There is a great myth in business perpetuated by leadership gurus, head hunters, pay consultants and even sometimes by the people who occupy some of the most senior corporate posts. It is the myth of the super-executive.

It is a compelling myth. We all know people in top jobs who have exceptional qualities, with the force of personality to drive through projects, the business acumen to make them succeed and the insight to spot a winner when they see one. Yet the super-executive is a myth all the same.

Some may believe that leadership itself is endowed with mythical properties. It is difficult to pin down the qualities needed for leading people and organizations. Among the most common we hear about these days are integrity, mental toughness, a sense of vision, an ability to listen, to see the big picture, to analyze concisely, to spot talent and to get the best out of others. We read too about humility, empathy and self-knowledge.

Accepting these many facets, we know instinctively that leadership cannot be mythical because we see it in action around us every day. We almost certainly demonstrate it ourselves, every single one of us. In the words of Warren Bennis, one of the world's most prolific writers on leadership, 'it is not simply about doing things right, but about "doing the right thing".'

But the responsibilities of leadership, whether leading a small team, a large corporate or a main board at group level, can weigh heavily when you are facing them alone. We all seek to do the right thing and sometimes we need help, particularly when our career journey is facing big change.

Change is everywhere today. Perhaps that has always been the case. Today, however, the change seems more noticeable – change in competition, markets, products, suppliers, legislation and in employment expectations.

There has probably never been a time in corporate history when the demands of executive leadership have been so onerous, or when the image of the super-executive has appeared so fragile.

There may be some individuals out there who are so brimming with confidence, so self-assured, so certain of the directions they need to take every single day that they can face the world alone. If so, I have yet to meet one of these hardy souls.

Much more common today in companies is the highly qualified, technically skilled, analytically sound executive who, in spite of all these exceptional qualities, is still in need of guidance.

This helps to explain why coaching has grown so much this past ten years or so. In our youths, coaching was something we experienced on the sports field. It was all about the acquisition, retention and improvement of specific technical skills, be it the golf swing, the tennis stroke or the bowling technique.

Then sports people began to look at psychology, since it was clear that technique alone was insufficient when competing at the highest levels. Golfers could suffer the yips, footballers could find they entered a barren spell in front of the goal, and tennis players could wilt when faced with an opponent they respected too much. Even the best players need to find what some have called their 'inner game'.

It was only a matter of time before coaching entered the executive suite. What goes for leading players in sport must go for professionals in other walks of life. In the corporate coaching arena, however, demands differ. It is not so much the need for the honing of technical skills that has defined executive coaching, but the need for guidance, the experienced hand on the elbow, the wise counsel, the independent voice and the impartial ear.

There must be thousands of individuals who can provide that sort of support. But the best coaching needs other skills too. Those who seek to step up to the plate and present themselves and their service as value-adding individuals must command the respect of their client companies and the trust of those they are asked to coach.

Creating the coaching proposition, then sustaining it and sharpening it as a significant force that adds real value to a business is what this book is all about. It's not enough to have wisdom or understanding if learning is not directed in a way that is going to be beneficial both to an individual and to the organization that is seeking to build its executive skills.

This is why the cumulative knowledge of Robin Linnecar and Peter Shaw, two of the UK's most experienced executive coaches, plus the insights generated by buyers of coaching and other coaches who they interviewed for the book, is directed here primarily at business effectiveness. But while their book is designed to enlighten organizations and individuals who can benefit from coaching, there is much to learn here also for coaches aspiring to operate at the highest levels.

The book is grounded in the practical experience of the authors and of those they consulted. It explains different coaching methods and themes and it outlines the benefits to be gained from coaching. It outlines the differences between coaching and mentoring and demonstrates how a coaching programme can be installed in a client organization.

This detailed structural breakdown of coaching programmes and how to get the most of them inside companies is one of the features of this book that differentiates it from others on the market. It spells out, in a clear, understandable narrative, the kind of objective setting, rules of engagement and measures companies should use to define success in a coaching relationship.

Most of all, however, it creates the proper context for coaching in the development of the modern organization.

Nothing on Earth can deliver the super-executive, the perfect, faultless decision-making machine, par excellence. Even the best people have their weaknesses. Great coaching, like great leadership, must seek continuous improvement in the teeth of those weaknesses.

Human frailty is a constant, but it is human strength and the power invested in self-knowledge that moulds the leadership for organizational success. The very best coaching has a deep and powerful role to play in building and maintaining this leadership excellence. But it must earn its place and win the trust of those who use it. This book provides the beacons that light the way.

Richard Donkin
Author and *Financial Times* columnist

Introduction

We believe passionately that coaching can have a dramatic effect on organizational success and individual performance. We are advocates of business coaching because we have seen its powerful effect in organizations of many different shapes and sizes. Whether the organization is a global conglomerate, a company operating in one country, a government department, a regional office, a charitable organization or a university, purposeful coaching of executives directed at specific challenges can be equally valuable.

Successful business coaching brings together meeting the needs of the employing organization and the individual. It impacts on the whole of an individual's life, with the clear outcome of increased effectiveness at work. It is unashamedly holistic. The more an individual sees different aspects of their life slotting in well together, the more effective they will be in their work situation.

Coaching is not a soft option. It is not cosy chats without purpose. Coaching is about focused conversations in which the individual feels both strongly supported and effectively challenged and stretched. The coachee will both be exhausted and invigorated by the process. The long-term result will be a strong sense of purpose, a clarity about aspirations and a set of pragmatic and focused next steps. Its impact on an organization will be leaders making better decisions, with the organization's performance improving as a consequence.

At the heart of coaching that works is effective engagement. This engagement has many strands. The starting point is the engagement between the coach and the client, enabling the client to engage effectively with business needs, themselves, their family and community responsibilities and their own futures. Engagement that is effective covers business, intellectual, emotional and transformational dimensions. The quality of engagement between coach and client feeds directly into the effective engagement of the client in delivering business needs.

The aim of this book is primarily to enable those wanting to invest in coaching to be able to do so in the most effective way, whether they are doing this as an organization or as an individual. It illustrates the impact coaching can have and identifies changes in leadership and management demands and expectations. We consider what a coachee gets out of coaching, different formats for coaching and its potential value at board level, including for the Chief Executive Officer, and for other individuals or groups such as new recruits or those who have just been promoted. We consider the difference between coaching and mentoring and the potential benefits that both can have, especially in combination. We look at how coaching programmes can be introduced effectively and how a leader might introduce coaching in their organization. We address the international dimension with many organizations looking to ensure that leadership is based on similar values throughout their global reach.

The book can be read right through, or specific chapters might be focused on for particular purposes. We have deliberately consulted widely in preparing this book and have included the views of clients and buyers of coaching. It is their perspective based on direct personal experience, together with our own experience, which has shaped our perspective in this book.

For us, coaching is the fulfilment of a lifetime of busy jobs. Robin has a wealth of experience from the private sector, having worked in Arthur Andersen, Shell International, Deloitte, Haskins and Sells, Coopers and Lybrand and KPMG. Peter worked in five government departments covering Education, Treasury, Employment, Transport and the Environment, and held three Director General posts within the Government. Both of us continue to have non-executive and part-time executive roles in addition to our coaching work.

We coach at senior levels in the public, private and voluntary sectors, cross-fertilizing ideas from our own leadership experience and from the wealth of conversations we now have with senior leaders. We coach because we love the work. We get a buzz from helping organizations work more effectively. There is such a joy in seeing individuals have the courage of their convictions stretched by the coaching and thereby become able to tackle difficult issues more effectively. We see ourselves as enablers. We share common values based on our belief that enabling somebody to integrate their physical, intellectual, emotional and spiritual wellbeing is crucial. Support and stretch come in equal measure.

We hope you will find this book both an inspiration and a quarry of suggestions. If coaching is already part of your armoury, this book can help you use it better. If coaching is new to you, try it but in a way that fits your needs and has a sharp focus on delivering the outcomes that are important to you.

Robin Linnecar and Peter Shaw
Pall Mall, London
February 2007

Chapter 1:

Effective Engagement

In this chapter we look at effective engagement as the common theme connecting the coach's work with the client to successful business outcomes. The quality of the engagement that the coach is able to generate is the major determinant of the success of the coaching. We look at:

- coaches who engage and clients who engage;
- characteristics of effective engagement between coach and client, including as a 'golden thread' the characteristics of 'respectful, listening, open-minded, flexible, supportive, challenging and forward looking';
- engagement as co-invention;
- varying the pace of engagement, covering thoughtful reflection, creative co-invention, purposeful dialogue and linking professional and personal priorities;
- engagement between the coach and the sponsor of the coaching; and
- where effective engagement can lead.

Coach, client and sponsor all have a part to play in ensuring the effectiveness of the coaching engagement.

Good coaching will feed directly through to the performance of an organization. The business case for coaching is based on individuals becoming more focused and successful in their work and contributing more effectively to corporate success. For this to happen, effective engagement is crucial at each step in the process, covering the relationship between coach and client, between the coach and business needs, and between clients and their own aspirations. The feedback loop to the success of the business is crucial to assessing the success of the coaching.

Coaches who engage

The following quotes are from buyers of coaching in a variety of organizations, who all put a strong emphasis on effective engagement between coach and client.

> *'Coaches must be grounded in commercial reality and be good at challenging in an appropriate way.'*
>
> Jill King, Linklaters

> *'Coaches should have experience and skills of their own to draw on. They must be able to hold the mirror up and be constructive.'*
>
> Philippa Charles, ABF Foods

> *'A good coach needs to listen and ask good questions. The coach must be able to articulate their area of specialism and be clear with which sort of people they work.'*
>
> Noel Hadden, Deutsche Bank

> *'Coaches must have high-quality interpersonal skills and be good at generating mutual confidence and quality relationships.'*
>
> Rob Edwards, UK Environment Agency

A consistent message is that coaches must work well with individuals and rapidly build an understanding of the environment in which they work. They need to understand the complexity of business life. It is crucial they bring organizational understanding and savvy. Common themes in these perspectives are understanding business reality, significant experience, strong 'interpersonal skills' and the ability to work with complexity.

Clients who engage

No effective coaching takes place unless the client engages with and is committed to the process. Here are some views from clients at the start of the engagement process with a coach:

> *'You were very helpful to a friend of mine when he took up a new FD role on the Board. I've now taken on this Managing Partner role, which I have never done before.'*
>
> Managing Partner, law firm

'I am the youngest on the Board. I want to become a credible candidate for CEO in the future. What can you do to help?'

CEO, Latin America, commercial company,
who was interviewing three coaches

'I want to establish priorities and plan for 12 months ahead. I want to bring about changes in people and culture and need to develop my client-influencing skills and relationship building. I need a sounding board.'

CEO, major consulting firm

At the outset, clients often do not know what coaching is about, but what they do know is that they want someone they can relate to and engage with because they are willing to 'give it a go'. They are committed to coaching in at least three areas:

- *Context*: e.g. taking on a new role.
- *Content*: e.g. either of a business nature, with the opportunity therefore to work through issues with someone jointly; or of a personal nature, in that they are not sure how to move forward and whether they have the skills or confidence to do so.
- *Challenge*: e.g. they need someone who can challenge and stretch them; take them out of their comfort zone so that they develop into someone bigger, better or more influential; and play 'at the top of their game'.

Characteristics of effective engagement between coach and client

The 'golden thread' running through effective engagement between coach and client includes the characteristics shown in Fig. 1.1.

Respectful includes trust and unconditional mutual regard. *Listening* is all about being fully present and giving someone sole, undivided attention. *Open-minded* is about banishing preconceived notions, being fully on the client's agenda and finding the point of need. *Flexible* is about varying the approach, pace and timing to fit the circumstances of the individual, using a variety of models. *Supportive* is about encouragement, emphasizing the positive and helping individuals keep up their energy. *Challenging* is about an engagement between equals where the coach is not deferential: it is about slicing through the dross and holding up a mirror to the client.

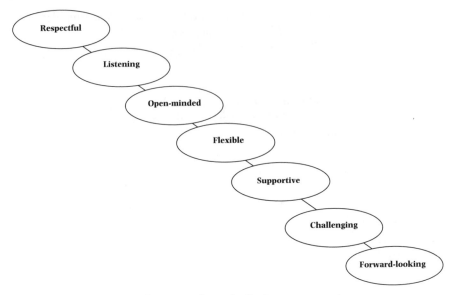

Fig. 1.1 The 'golden thread' running through effective engagement

Forward looking is about a relentless focus on the future, whatever past or current travails there have been.

Effective engagement between coach and client involves various areas (see Fig. 1.2). Effective engagement requires the coach to have a grounding in the *business needs* and priorities of the organization. This does not mean the coach will have worked in precisely the same situation, but direct per-

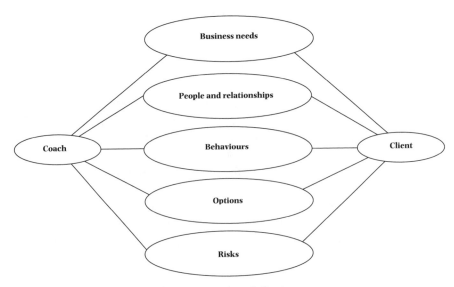

Fig. 1.2 Effective engagement between coach and client

sonal experience of a similar leadership position will be immensely helpful. It helps root the conversations in business reality. Using an analogy from sport, good sports coaches do not have to have been the champion at the same level, but they do need to have been 'up there', living and breathing the joys and pressures.

The good coach will bring to the conversation a firm understanding of *people and relationships*. There will be a natural empathy with different types of people, coupled with a hard edge about what helps individuals focus and deliver more effectively. An understanding of behaviours will be an essential underpinning to the dialogue, to help the coach bring new insights and perspectives.

Good coaching conversation will be engaging, with *options* and *risks*. There will be the private space to explore topics in a measured and emotional way. The coach is pointing out angles or implications, but the client is shaping the options and working through later stages. A crucial contribution from the business coach is to help an individual engage with the issues which are most important and to think through the risks effectively. Understanding risks well is possibly the most valuable perspective a coach can bring.

Engagement about business needs will be at different levels, depending on the responsibilities of the client. The more senior the client, the more the discussion will be at a strategic level. But whatever the seniority of the individual, a common theme is likely to be working at identifying key priorities.

These are four important levels of engagement between coach and client as shown in Fig. 1.3.

Factual is about being on the same page in terms of information. It is about having a significant understanding of the background and the context. It is not having an encyclopaedic knowledge of an area, but does involve a good understanding of the key parameters and levers.

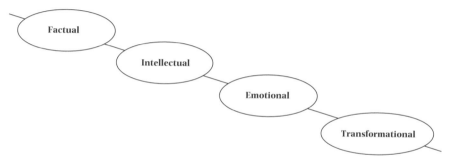

Fig. 1.3 The four levels of engagement

Intellectual is about being able to talk about issues on equal terms in a robust way: it includes seeing the policy and operational consequences of different actions.

Emotional is about an openness of human strengths and frailties. It is creating a relationship whereby the client is willing to be open about their emotional reactions and to move on, through recognizing what they find difficult and how they want to develop their own capacity for courage and resilience. Emotional reactions in leaders may be getting in the way of the individual's clear, authentic leadership: if the coach can help bring clarity, a road block to progress can be removed.

Transformational is about a quality of coaching discourse which results in the client viewing themselves and their situation in an entirely different way. The coach has to be prepared to read their own emotional reactions in a coaching discussion, using them as a barometer of the impact the client has on others.

In the best of coaching discussions there is the creativity of two people working well together. There is focused questioning and dialogue when the overall result is more than the sum of the parts. The interaction leads to creative and dynamic progress towards new solutions. Sometimes when the coach and client look back, they are surprised by the progress that has taken place.

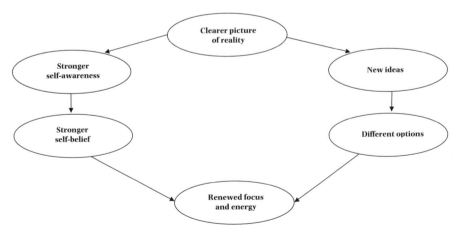

Fig. 1.4 Engagement as a co-invention of ideas and possibilities

Engagement as co-invention

In our view, coaching is not the coach just asking questions and listening, nor is it the coach providing solutions: the best engagements include a co-invention of ideas and possibilities (see Fig. 1.4).

Co-invention has to start from a *clear picture of reality*, grounded in facts and in a good understanding of the context. Co-invention may then travel down two tracks. On the left-hand side of Fig. 1.4 is the personal dimension, covering *self-awareness* and *self-belief*, where psychologically based approaches can be a valuable aid. On the right-hand side of the diagram is the business dimension, where creative discussion leads to *new ideas* and *different options*. The result of exploring both dimensions is *renewed focus and energy*.

For engagement to happen effectively, you cannot have a rigid process or a forced fit. The engagement between coach and coachee has to evolve. In a long-term coaching relationship, the engagement will have gone through many different phases. Coaching is like going on a route through a forest where the terrain varies: sometimes the coach and client are travelling together, but through very different terrain; on other occasions, they will be going through similar landscape and dealing on a regular basis with issues that the client finds most difficult.

Varying the pace of engagement

The engagement between coach and client is always client focused, but is likely to have a range of different dimensions (see Fig 1.5).

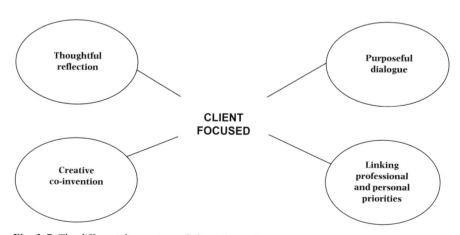

Fig. 1.5 The different dimensions of client-focused engagement

Thoughtful reflection may well be looking at the implications of past and current events. It is looking at the context and assessing the relative importance of events. It is standing back and considering how important something is 'in the great scheme of things'. *Purposeful dialogue* is likely to be focused on a particular issue, looking at possible action and risks. It is moving to specific measurable next steps and outcomes.

Creative co-invention is considering in a more open way new approaches and dimensions, possibly with a long-term focus. *Linking professional and personal priorities* is about always coming back to an individual reflecting on their own values and interlinking the vision and responsibilities they have at both a professional and personal level.

The coaching conversations must always enable the client to engage effectively with the worlds that are most important to them. Key elements are illustrated in Fig 1.6.

The rationale for business coaching is helping to meet business needs, but the four dimensions in the diagram need to be in reasonable harmony if an individual is going to make a maximum contribution to meeting business needs.

Individual clients need to be able to engage with themselves in terms of understanding their strengths and weaknesses, and have enough self-knowledge to enable them to move on. Clients need to be conscious about the relative importance for them of the family and community dimension, both in terms of understanding themselves and in terms of clarity about their personal priorities. It also helps if the individual is willing to engage

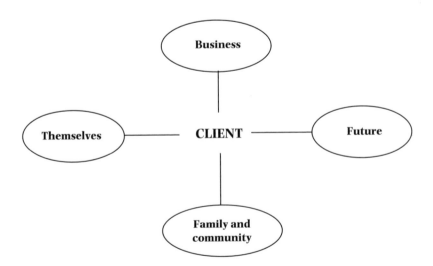

Fig. 1.6 Key elements of coaching conversations

with different options about the future and is willing to sometimes remove blinkers that might be constraining their view of future possibilities.

Part of individuals engaging with themselves is understanding the complex web within them that brings together their drivers, frailties, fears and aspirations. It is the fascinating interlinking of these different aspects of personality that makes engaging with yourself as an individual absorbing. It must not become excessively self-indulgent. It needs to be an engagement that helps the individual move on to more effectively engage themselves with their work and personal priorities.

Engagement between coach and sponsor

Coaching is part of a three-way relationship between coach, client and sponsor (see Fig 1.7).

The sponsor is the lead person within the organization employing the client. This might be the CEO, HR Director or the Line Manager, depending on who is taking the primary responsibility in ensuring the success of the coaching. Often all are involved to some degree.

The engagement between coach and sponsor is important in ensuring the success of the coaching work, without in any way affecting the confidentiality of the relationship between the coach and client. This engagement might cover the areas shown in Fig.1.8.

Where the coach understands the business needs and opportunities from the perspective of the sponsor, they can more readily focus the coaching work. Briefing about the organization in terms of its structures, organiza-

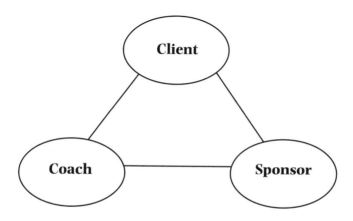

Fig.1.7 Coaching as a three-way relationship

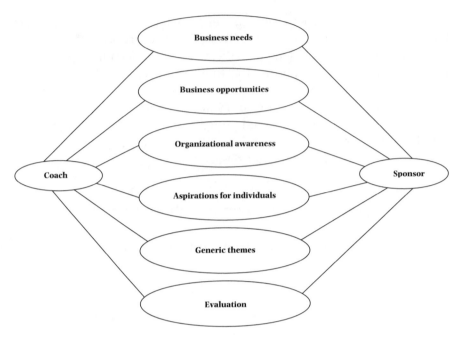

Fig. 1.8 The engagment between coach and sponsor

tional behaviours and culture can provide a valuable context for the coach. Being aware of the organization's perspective on an individual in terms of capabilities and potential is an important starting point.

Effective engagement with the sponsor includes feedback of generic themes where a number of clients are involved, and the evaluation of the outcomes of the coaching work. Part of effective engagement is the willingness of the sponsor to change their mind about an individual when there has been a transformation in an individual's confidence and competence. The sponsor needs to believe that coaching can work and not be fixed into a rigid perspective about an individual's capabilities!

Effective engagement internationally

Effective engagement by coaches will take account of both cultural and linguistic differences as shown in Fig. 1.9. Economic drivers mean that cross-cultural and international working is essential. Coaches who are internationally aware can enable individuals to cope effectively with cultural and linguistic differences and ensure that economic drivers for co-operation are used effectively. Using modern communication well and ensuring virtual

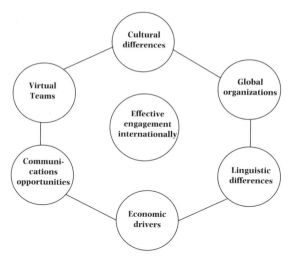

Fig. 1.9 Effective engagement internationally

teams are successful pushes the business leader into new and innovative ways of engaging. Elements of effective engagement internationally are illustrated in Fig.1.9.s

Where can effective engagement lead?

Our thesis is that good business outcomes require the client to be engaged on the right activities in a focused way. Achieving this depends on effective engagement of coach and client: engagement that is factual, intellectual, emotional and transformational, with phases of thoughtful reflection, purposeful dialogue, creative co-invention and the linking of professional and personal priorities alongside a positive mental attitude. This book now looks at effective engagement through a range of different perspectives. Engagement is not about 'one size fits all'; it is about a flow of conversation that moves an agenda on at a pace which fits the needs of the client and enables them to be energized by the process.

Chapter 2:

The Impact of Coaching

This chapter addresses the impact of coaching covering:
- examples of the impact of coaching;
- perspectives from individuals who have extensive experience of introducing and buying coaching in a range of sectors, covering the value-added they want to see out of coaching ;
- the potential benefits of coaching for organizations;
- the potential benefits of coaching for individuals;
- key questions to ask on the benefits of coaching; and
- the cost benefits of coaching.

In particular, it sets out a framework for assessing the potential benefits of coaching for an organization and for individuals, covering business outcomes, people and relationships and behaviours. The key questions asked and benefits of coaching described provide a framework for organizations and individuals to consider when embarking upon business coaching.

Business coaching is not for the faint-hearted. Quality coaching conversations are not fireside rambles going nowhere. Effective coaching is focused and productive. Good coaching is based on a wealth of experience from the coach, the strong support of the employing organization and the clear commitment of the individual.

Examples of the impact of coaching

Coaching should not be entered into lightly because, when done well, it will have a lasting impact not only on the commitment and focus of individuals in a particular situation but also on their capability and personal ambition.

It can unleash new energies and tap into hidden resources. John Harper, a managing director in an investment bank working in the international retail area, says of the coaching:

> 'I found the meetings were more structured than I would have antici-pated and, following a certain amount of drilling down, measurable action points fell naturally out of the discussions. Interestingly these action points were mainly business-orientated and have stretched my performance. This would not have happened without coaching.'

A newly-promoted member of the senior team in a UK government agency, Adele Westcott, said of her coaching for a crucial interview:

> 'If it were not for the coach's challenge, I would not have prepared prop-erly. This is a lesson I will take with me throughout my career.'

John is a Board director in a FTSE 250 company in the UK. Highly experi-enced, he embarked on a process of moving the organization from func-tional business lines to regional lines (and thus multi-functional lines). His perspective is as follows:

> 'Coaching enabled me to stand back and see the critical steps in manag-ing change and then work through them. Not least was the relation-ship with my CEO and, by addressing that, we moved forward much faster.'

Many of those who have experienced coaching refer to the development of self-confidence and a greater sense of courage of their convictions and a more focused impact. Portia Ragnauth was appointed the Chief Crown Prosecutor for a county in the north of England in 2004, with responsibil-ity for the Regional Office. Portia is a dynamic and energetic young lady. She commented that:

> 'The coaching was so important to me in getting established in a very different role. It helped me focus and prepare for difficult meetings and situations. It forced me to look at the bigger picture. It gave me space to work through precisely what I wanted to do. It helped ensure that I had the courage of my own convictions.'

Making a personal impact is equally important in the public, private and voluntary sectors. Rafik Kaabi has had a fascinating career within Shell. With a mixed European and North African background, he brings a unique international perspective to his work. A lot of the coaching related to interview skills and personal impact more generally, with a thrust on sharpening his focus, developing clarity and raising confidence. He commented that,

> 'The coaching forced me to sharpen my presentation. I became much clearer in all I said. I was far less apologetic. The coach was relentless in helping me ensure I was always clear, positive and engaged in everything I said.'

Nick Brown describes a coaching relationship that has been important to him for close to 15 years. During this period, Nick has moved from the public sector into the private sector and is now Chief Executive of SERCO Integrated Transport. He says of the coaching:

> 'Coaching has helped me in handling transitions from one job to the next. It has enabled me to have the right mindset in preparing for a move and to have an effective focus on execution once in it. The coaching has specifically identified training gaps different to organizational needs. It has helped me focus on career management, covering long-term needs at a strategic level and short-term requirements at a tactic level. The coaching has not meant that I have taken a different view. But it has helped me place boundaries around problems so I deal with them in a more structured way, working through the consequences of different options. The coaching discussions have helped concrete my thinking after working through tricky issues.'

Nick describes the benefit of coaching as raising his level of self-confidence and, as a consequence, his level of competence. It has equipped him to coach and mentor his staff effectively. He says that it has been most helpful when he has been working on a big change management agenda, where it has enabled him to move on from uncertainty.

He describes the essential characteristic of a good coach as:

> 'Someone who has your best interests at heart at both a business and personal level. Someone who will drive, challenge and support you and who will help you find the catalyst that makes effective change happen.'

The benefits of coaching in these illustrations result from the intensity of the one-to-one engagement, with practical steps to embed the learning and rigorous self-appraisal a crucial part of the process.

Perspectives from individuals who have used coaching in major organizations

In writing this book, we have drawn from the perspectives of a range of people with extensive experience of introducing and buying coaching. We have selected four from the private sector and three from the public sector, namely:

- Noel Hadden, the Director of Learning and Development at Deutsche Bank in London;
- Hilary Douglas, the Chief Operating Officer for the UK Department of Trade and Industry, who has been the Board Member responsible for HR in six government organizations;
- Jim McCaffery, who is HR Director of the Lothian Health Authority and has extensive experience in both the private and public sectors;
- Rob Edwards, who is Manager of the Management Development Team at the UK Environment Agency and has introduced and managed coaching in both the public and private sectors;
- Jill King, who is HR Director for Linklaters, a leading international law firm;
- John Bailey, who is responsible for decisions about buying in coaching at a professional service firm, KPMG; and
- Philippa Charles, who is the Director of Executive Development at AB Foods, an international food company.

The perspective from their wide experience of both the private and public sectors is as follows.

What is the value-added you particularly want to see out of coaching?

'When it works well, it is the Number 1 development opportunity after experience on the job. When it is done badly, it is a waste of time and can be damaging. Coaching is the ultimate tailored development solution. Because of the opportunity cost for business of people being away from their desk, focused coaching at the right time and right place is very powerful.'

Noel Hadden

'The organization paying the bill must see a difference in the individual's performance or a stretch in their potential. While the individual might be looking for someone to talk to in a confidential way, the organization must be hard-headed about what the benefits are going to be out of coaching.'

Hilary Douglas

'Coaching must lead to focused self-reflection. It is most effective when it is helping somebody who is doing well; however, what has worked well for individuals before isn't necessarily going to work as well in the future. This is particularly when style needs to change or people need to adopt roles or organizational dynamics. Individuals need to be pressed to think through what made them successful and what now needs to change in a more senior or demanding role.'

Jim McCaffery

'The value-added in some cases will be addressing immediate managerial challenges, where coaching can be used in a speedy and targeted way. It can also have important transformational value-added effects, helping senior people to understand themselves better: but the coaching always needs to be targeted in relation to delivering business needs that are most important.'

Rob Edwards

'Coaching can focus on real issues because it is about targeted conversations as they arise in real time. To be fully effective, coaching needs to be blended in with other types of development.'

Jill King

'I particularly want to see coaching as an integral part of an organization's culture that feeds through to creativity. It is the cultural benefits that are important. The key issue is the extent to which coaching has helped an individual address an issue and develop more broadly.'

John Bailey

A consistent theme is that the value-added needs to contribute to an organization's leadership capability. It must be wider than benefits for one individual. If coaching can lead to successful behavioural change in a leader it will have a knock on effect on raising leadership capability more generally and enabling the organization to meet its goals more effectively.

In what situations do you think coaching can be most beneficial?

'We use coaching for very senior people, with complex jobs that are global, who are time-constrained, running complex businesses operating around the clock. The coach can be a sounding board bringing an independent perspective to specific issues with no axes to grind. Coaching can help with high performers, especially ones with behavioural edges that can be derailing factors. Where individuals are moving into more complex roles, coaching through the first 90 days can make a significant difference. The use of 360° feedback is an almost essential part of the process, whereby a mirror is held up to the individual about the impact they are having: this is a very helpful way of enabling somebody to begin to fulfil their potential. The net effect is that we retain our best people, drive performance upwards, and improve the bottom line. Ensuring people's behaviours are consistent with the overall values of the organization has a trickle-down effect that can be marked: the benefit of the investment in coaching is not just therefore in the individuals who receive the coaching.'

Noel Hadden

'As well as helping high-potential people, coaching can make a big difference for those not performing to their full potential, who need one-to-one work to enable them to focus on what they can do differently in terms of raising self-awareness and self-confidence. The key test is, will there be a difference in an individual's performance that warrants the investment?'

Hilary Douglas

'Coaching is most effective well before there are any problems. Its biggest impact can be in helping people getting ready for promotion or when taking on a new challenging role. I've seen it be very effective when someone who has been a good performer has slipped a bit and needs help to recover their focus and their energy. The key thing is getting coaching in early in a focused way.'

Jim McCaffery

'Its biggest effects have been with the top leadership team and those with high potential. I recently saw a member of our Talent Pool change significantly. He had profound issues about the way he thought and felt and demonstrated an overly deferential approach, which was getting in the way of his credibility. The coaching relationship helped him get through the ritual dance that he so often engaged in. The progress has been clear and measurable with both the individual and the project he is leading benefiting substantially.'

Rob Edwards

'It is particularly useful in two classic situations. Firstly, it is useful with a role transition, when somebody has been promoted or is taking on new responsibilities. Having somebody work with an individual, helping them to think through the challenges they are going to face and how they are going to reinvent themselves is invaluable. The other classic situation is where somebody is going through a situation of organizational change, where senior people need to guide others through the situation. Coaching in this context can address the situation of somebody being lonely at the top, where it is difficult to find somebody to talk to on equal terms. A sounding board when going through major change can be very helpful.'

Jill King

'Coaching can be most successful when somebody is going into a new job where there is little or no precedent. A coach can help somebody develop a new role or stock-take at particular points, weighing up options and developing strategies for the future.'

John Bailey

'Three key areas are remedial, transition and enhancement. Remedial coaching can provide genuine tools and techniques to help an individual address issues that are getting in the way. There can be improved self-awareness and impact on others, with influencing in stakeholder management skills greatly improved. In a transition situation, particularly a first general management role, a coach can provide an external sounding board. A coach can help ensure clear outcomes through being a listening ear and a guiding hand. Enhancement coaching is about fine-tuning and enhanced self-awareness. A coach can enable somebody to build on their strengths and can help them work through unintended consequences of their strengths.'

Philippa Charles

These individuals come from widely different organizations, but there is a commonality of view about some of the potential benefits of coaching. The benefit varies depending on the individual. Some of the dimensions include helping people get up to speed quickly if they are new to a role. It can be particularly useful in building relationships when progress gets blocked. Relationship building comes up time and time again as a prime reason for coaching. Effective development of influencing styles can be one of the immediate results. The heart of beneficial coaching is enabling people to look objectively at the effect of their behaviours and then put constructive measures in place.

Coaching is seen as a tailored solution with stretching conversations that allow somebody to have a sounding board at key moments. They see coaching working in a variety of contexts but with some common themes about the value of coaching for people in transition or needing to develop leadership skills in a situation where they may have limited support from others.

Potential benefits of coaching for organizations

Three key benefits for organizations can be seen in Fig 2.1. Taking each of these in turn:

Business outcomes

This might include:
- moving the organization forward at a pace and in a direction which is to its competitive advantage;
- stronger support behind major culture-change initiatives;
- a stronger alignment between an individual's objectives and the overall strategic objectives of the organization;

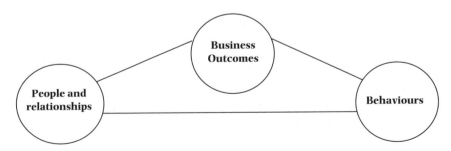

Fig. 2.1 Key benefits for organizations

- greater self-awareness of the impact an individual is having, both on the success of the business and on the people with whom they work;
- focus on individual development which takes place at a time most convenient to the individual with minimum detrimental impact on their work; and
- good generic feedback to the organization in an anonymized form of issues that need to be tackled.

People and relationships

This might include:

- greater levels of skills awareness and people deploying their strengths to optimal effect;
- greater focus on succession planning and talent development
- relationship issues identified and tackled effectively;
- teams operating more smoothly with a much stronger strategic sense;
- stronger corporate relationships across the organization.

Behaviours

This might include:

- consistency of leadership decisions and behaviours;
- difficult challenges faced up to and tackled within the organization;
- much better use of time and energy by senior leaders;
- the surety that individuals are receiving focused feedback via and from the coach in terms of their personal impact; and
- the giving of an employee benefit which enables an individual to better interrelate their personal and work priorities and commitments.

There are some potential disadvantages for organizations encouraging business coaching. Because of the time commitment, there is an opportunity cost: the test is whether the results of the coaching are evident in an individual's performance. The financial cost can be significant: one-to-one coaching is inevitably expensive because of the time commitment. Employing coaches with top-level experience as leaders means recognizing that experience in the rates that are paid. Those who have had the benefit of coaching may well become more assertive and show much more courage in their own convictions: the crucial dimension is how the organization uses this assertiveness and courage to the best effect.

Looking with a coach at their life priorities could in certain cases mean that individuals decide to focus on other priorities or move on: but it is in the organization's interests that an individual's motivation is tested out in a safe environment. If an individual is becoming less positive about their role, it is better that this is worked through in structured conversations with next steps being reflected on in a way which helps somebody to move on without ill will.

Potential benefits for individuals

The potential benefits for individuals cover the same territory as the benefits for organizations, namely: business outcomes, people and relationships and behaviours. The benefits can include:

Business outcomes

- clarifying the vision or overall strategy: e.g. working from the organization's strategic purpose into clarifying a personal vision consistent with both the organization's aspirations and the individual's contribution;
- working through priorities: e.g. being very clear where the individual's contribution can be at its most value-added, distinguishing between important and urgent tasks and helping to rank them in importance;
- better time management: e.g. looking at past and future diaries and working through the most effective use of time; and thereby becoming clearer about how best they can add value;
- increased competence in particular skills: e.g. presentation skills, interview technique or building relationships;
- ensuring the best use is made of courses: e.g. by linking a course an individual goes on with the issues being worked on in coaching; and
- integrating short- and long-term aspirations: e.g. working through where a current job is leading.

People and relationships

- ensuring work relationships are at their most productive: e.g. self-assessing the effectiveness of existing relationships and developing strategies for improving relationships; and
- making the most effective use of staff, e.g. working through issues like delegation, training and career development.

Behaviours

- enabling an individual to consistently give of their best so that their leadership messages and behaviours are consistently as they want them to be;

- increased confidence in tackling individual challenges: e.g. the coaching discussions provide a safe environment in which there can be open discussion about a particular issue, with the individual able to rehearse the approach they want to take;
- tackling the most difficult problems: e.g. the coaching discussion enables these difficult issues to be aired honestly and sound next steps developed to tackle them;
- working on very personal considerations like an individual's presence in meetings and personal impact: e.g. using assessment by the coach or through 360° feedback; and
- integrating work and life priorities and time: e.g. looking at an individual's overall life priorities and helping them define the relationship between the time commitments for work and life.

Key questions on the benefits of coaching

Where you are thinking of introducing or developing coaching within your organization, key questions to work through are:

- what benefits do you want to see out of the coaching work?
- what are the particular challenges that you would like to see tackled in the coaching conversations?
- how much investment of both money and senior leadership time are you prepared to invest into coaching?
- how prepared are you to take advantage of the results of coaching if individuals develop much stronger leadership skills, with increased courage of their convictions and a more focused impact?
- how willing are you to receive generic feedback from the results of the coaching work?
- will you be prepared to modify your methods or values if the unleashed potential amongst senior staff becomes a powerful force for good?

For the individual who is thinking upon embarking upon coaching the issues are:

- how willing are you to be challenged and stretched in coaching conversations?
- are there difficult areas which you seldom enter into, for which coaching would be likely to be of positive benefit?
- are you willing to engage with the coach in a creative way: is co-invention an attractive option?

- are you willing to open up in the confidentiality of a coaching discussion in a way which may mean that you have to address inconsistencies in your own attitudes and behaviour?
- do you seriously want to use your time and energy more effectively, even though this might initially be uncomfortable?
- are you clear where you want to make a step-change in your contribution to the business?

The cost benefits of coaching

We have outlined above some of the benefits of coaching to an organization in terms of business outcomes. A lot of this is qualitative, but to what extent can it be quantitative? Does the coaching of a Sales Director lead directly to an increase in the revenue line of that organization?

An article in the Manchester Review 2001 Volume 6 Number 1 *Maximising the Impact of Executive Coaching* came to the conclusion that there was a 5.7-fold benefit in terms of return on investment in currency terms, averaging nearly $100,000.

A recent piece of work on cost benefits is the paper by Gavin Dagley published in the November 2006 edition of the *International Coaching Psychology Review*. He did structured interviews with 17 HR professionals to elicit their perceptions of the overall efficacy of executive coaching, which in total covered over 1000 individuals: 11% of coaching programmes were rated as outstandingly successful, 47% as very successful, 28% as moderately successful and only 14% as marginally or not successful.

To make a precise cost-benefit link is not straightforward, but there are at least three ways of getting at such a cost benefit.

- *Skill enhancement* – in our experience, many senior executives and board members have the opportunity to attend business school courses and seminars covering several weeks at Harvard, INSEAD and other such national or international venues. While the networking benefits to the individual, the raising of general business awareness and knowledge increases are evident, there is often a need for coaching to ensure that learning gets *practised* in the workplace on return. If an executive needs to develop themselves as a leader and adopt the skills of authenticity or implementing change, or any other skill, then focused, dedicated coaching time at £X may well be more valuable in meeting the need than attendance at a programme in a business school, taking the individual out of the workplace for longer periods, with cost multiples of £Y. Weighing the costs and relative merits of courses or coaching is important.

- *Behavioural change* – efficiency and effectiveness can be measured in different ways. An executive's ability to chair a meeting more efficiently (skill) is akin to their ability to motivate and enthuse colleagues rather than create inefficiencies by being demotivating and authoritarian. Coaching in behavioural change can be assessed through 360° feedback before and after coaching.
- *Accelerated development* – recent research has shown that around two in every five new CEOs fail within the first 18 months of appointment. If coaching can help avoid that situation, the resultant head-hunter fees and other costs will not be incurred so regularly.

The impact of coaching: a personal story

Phil Hodkinson is the Finance Director of HBOS and has worked with a coach for a number of years. Phil identified three particular focuses of coaching which are relevant for him:

- Very specific coaching in technical areas;
- Helping to build strengths or addressing less strong areas where the focus is on a broader management skill set; i.e. generic to role rather than specific to role;
- Contextual coaching where there is the opportunity with the coach to rehearse ways to address issues in the organization: this coaching is based on understanding the dynamics in the organization and rehearsing ways to take forward particular issues.

Phil comments:

> 'It is very easy to repeat what has been successful in the past. Coaching has widened my perspective. There are many more ways of playing the game: coaching has brought this alive. There is more than one way of skinning a cat: coaching has helped me identify with more of a range of alternatives. My coach has a fantastic ability to suggest a range of alternatives: he has built up an understanding of the personalities in my world and the way they might respond.'

In terms of the nature of the engagement between coach and client, Phil makes the following comments:

'The first year was an investment on both our parts. My coach met colleagues, so when we talked about challenges he knew the individuals. He could identify conflicting and reinforcing perspectives of individuals. The anonymized 360° feedback gave me valuable feedback. I share thoughts with my coach I haven't shared with anyone else. His perspective is always in my best interest. Every year I have an offsite meeting with my coach when we go further than trusted adviser role to helping me find my level of ambition. It has helped to clarify my thinking over the next few years. It has been a catalyst for a career/life plan.'

Phil describes the results of the coaching in the following way:

'I believe I am now able to influence more powerfully in a greater range of fora. There was one way I played events: there is now a greater range. As a consequence I am more influential in the boardroom. One of the ways I can be influential is better networking externally, enabling me to speak with more impact internally. My coach helped me to develop the strength to contribute to a broader range of subjects and the ability to link issues together.'

In terms of the benefits of coaching for his own staff and the outcomes he seeks, Phil's perspective is:

'You need to be clear what type of coaching is needed. Most of my direct reports are very senior people so taking their technical skills and employing them in a wider range of situations is important. The main benefit is for an individual to develop the ability to know when to influence, when to stand back and how to read a situation better.'

Conclusion

Coaching makes a tremendous difference for sports players; business coaching can have just as big an impact on leaders in any sector provided it is used wisely. The rest of this book is based on the premise that making the most effective use of coaching through encouraging effective engagement will be hugely beneficial to any organization or individual.

Chapter 3:

Coaching in Context: Changes in Leadership and Management Demands and Expectations

This chapter looks at the changes in leadership demands and expectations which create the environment in which coaching operates. It covers:

- the changing context of leadership;
- the leadership development continuum, which covers traditional, modern and emergent leadership;
- the changing relationship between individual and organization context;
- the changing demands and expectations on leaders;
- the relevance of strategic leadership frameworks for coaching; and
- creating the right environment for effective leadership development.

An internet search of the phrases 'management development' and 'leadership development' produces 1420 million hits and 414 million hits respectively. If the words 'executive coaching' are included alongside each phrase, the hit rates come down to 29 and 26 million. While there might be a big debate about management versus leadership, the implication is that coaching is equally useful in either context.

This kind of internet search is not scientifically rigorous, but the truth contained within it is that the context in which business coaching finds itself is very wide. Coaching is but one part of a leader's development. It is one tool in the kitbag of tools for development available to leaders to enable them to be more effective and achieve their potential. Leaders can choose to use these tools or not. Some organizations will insist they are used; a lot will leave it up to the leaders to self-develop.

Coaching is increasingly seen as the ultimate development tool, or rather redevelopment tool. Someone who has potential (doesn't everybody?)

needs development; someone who has to perform (doesn't everybody?) needs the opportunity to enhance that performance. Either way, coaching can be seen to be the answer and the ultimate weapon in the management and leadership development armoury. This is fine provided coaching is used effectively.

Business coaching has become a distinct professional area within the industry of coaching. The coaching world is still evolving into many forms, e.g. life coaching and 'agony aunt' coaching in various magazines, at one end of the spectrum, through career coaching, skills coaching, to coaching for performance, transition coaching and executive and leadership coaching. We place business coaching as a distinct professional area within coaching with a firm focus on raising business performance.

The context of leadership

Coaching needs to be put in the context of how leadership is evolving. In a study of leadership you can start at any point in history – Moses leading the children of Israel out of Egypt into the Promised Land, Achilles leading his armies against the Trojans, the host guiding the Pilgrims to Canterbury.

The idea that leadership was something that could be developed emerged in the second half of the 20th Century when the approaches of leaders like Hitler, Churchill and Franco were analysed in depth. Blanchard's *Situational Leadership*, John Adair's *Action Centred Leadership* and Robert Greenleaf's *Servant Leadership* have all become highly influential books on leadership. An excellent summary of the modern theories is set out in *In Search of Leaders* by Hilarie Owen, published by Wiley in 2000.

One of our colleagues, Nicola Haskins, in a dissertation carried out at the University of Surrey in 2005, identifies three broad trends in the management and leadership literature that, building on themselves over time, can be depicted as in Fig. 3.1:

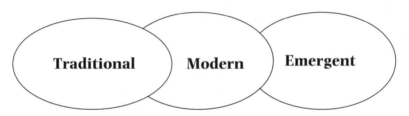

Fig. 3.1 Three broad trends in management and leadership literature

The leadership development continuum

- The **Traditional** leadership model focuses on the attributes possessed by a single leader, in which it is the skills within the individual that are emphasized. Traditional leadership development practices are based on 360° feedback mechanisms and developed through one-to-one coaching.
- The **Modern** leadership model suggests that leadership is something which is negotiated between individuals and, as such, relies heavily on interpersonal influence. The focus is on the team and the building of networked relationships; hence the goal is on developing interpersonal intelligence and relational skills and the most effective development interventions are team building and team coaching.
- The **Emergent** leadership model, which, as its name suggests, is at the cutting edge of leadership thinking, expands the notion of leadership away from the leader-led principle tone to one which embraces all levels of the system as in Fig. 3.1. The thinking here is that, in an increasingly interconnected and complex world, more and more people are needed to interpret complex information; no one person can do it all, so what is needed is to develop connected leadership across an organization. The focus now shifts away from the individual or the small team to developing the organization's collective leadership capacity; hence the terminology changes from 'leader' to 'leadership' development with a more transpersonal focus.

The key thing Haskins points out, however, is that it is not a question of either/or with these models. Each stage includes and transcends the previous stage, so organizations need to pay attention to both the individual and the collective leadership development.

These trends can be seen in the writings of Drath (2001), Pernick (2001), Centre for Creative Leadership (CCL) (2004), Senge (2002) and others. More recent publications bear out Haskins' analysis, such as Rob Goffee and Gareth Jones in *Why should anyone be led by You* (2006) which examines what it takes to be an authentic leader. Business coaching has to be seen as operating within this evolving leadership context and can enable success to be more readily assured across all three dimensions.

We now look at the changing context of leadership from an individual and a corporate organizational viewpoint.

	Traditional	Modern	Emergent
Leadership model	'Heroic'	Interpersonal influence	Relational dialogue
	Leader + followers	Team-based leadership	Connected leadership
Development focus	Individual	Teams	Everyone (organization stakeholders)
Type of intervention	360° feedback	Team building	Dialogue
	One-to-one coaching	Team coaching	Sense-making
	Behavioural observation	Action learning	Storytelling
Targeted outcomes	Intrapersonal	Interpersonal	Transpersonal
	Skills within individual	Links between individuals	Going beyond individuals
	Self-awareness	Empathy	Allowing the whole to emerge
	Self-management	Understanding of others	

Fig. 3.2 The leadership development continuum. Based on work by Drath (2001), CCL (2004), Pernick (2001) and Day (2001)

Individual context

Leaders grow up within organizations. It is a feature of work in the 21st century that individuals will have worked for lots of different organizations and will not be in the same organization throughout their working lives. As a result, individuals will be individual kaleidoscopes of many different cultures, systems, natures and qualities. Just as a kaleidoscope shows constantly changing, brightly coloured figures, so an executive exhibits a whole range of 'sides' depending on personality, situation and context. Event or occurrence A, B, or C will trigger an interaction of background, culture, system or nature in the individual leader. Executives and leaders need this flexibility and need to be aware of its importance.

How many times have we heard someone say, 'I have never seen that side of John or Mary before. It quite surprised me!'? Something or someone had 'turned' their individual kaleidoscope and a new pattern of behaviour had emerged. We are not suggesting that executives *only* respond to their environments and behave in some particular way as a result, but understanding this interrelation of individual characteristics is a key starting point. Looking at experiences and influences as 'compound' rather than 'single' is essential.

A simple analogy with sport might help. The purpose of the coach in sport is to bring out the best in the individual's or team performance and to both sustain and enhance that. For any one athlete or team, bringing out performance is just one part of their development. There will be a need to look at managing the championships or next venue as well as pick which event is best to enter. The coach may look at technique, style, breathing, diet, muscle trim, stamina and a whole range of other considerations. There will also be a need to look at tactics and strategy on the track for the event itself. The individual needs to be fully aware of all these aspects of their situation. Hence a coach who is looking at the athlete's technique alone is looking at but one small part of the overall picture of the individual.

Organizational context

An individual leader works within an organization and the environment in which it operates. From the sporting world, Mike Brearley, former England cricket captain, set out views on this in his book, *The Art of Captaincy*, which continue to be highly pertinent. For him, a leader's contribution in cricket is crucial because there are three overriding considerations:

- the time span of the game and the changing tempo within it;
- the variation in conditions which are beyond the leader's control (weather, nature of pitch, character of umpires, crowds' temperament, etc.); and
- the variety of roles within a single team: 'A captain must get the best out of his team by helping them to play together without suppressing flair and uniqueness.'

An organization within which a leader works has a purpose, a strategy, a business or sector within which it operates, and an environment that impacts on everything it does (markets, pricing, resource allocation and availability, etc). The coach could spend a lot of time thinking about the individual executive's 'technique' as with the athlete analogy. The question of what type of wider development is appropriate will be important, such as on-the-job experience, training courses, senior management programmes, university or business school programmes, secondments, postings, projects, assignments or promotion. The wider considerations referred to above will impact on the individual executive's development and will take on different levels of relative importance depending on organizational needs.

The changing relationship between individual and organizational context

Coaching finds itself in a very different global world. In the 20th Century, organizations nurtured their employees and groomed their leaders from apprentice through the hierarchy. Partners who entered professional firms (e.g. lawyers and accountants) as articled clerks evolved to partnership within the same organization. Gold watches and carriage clocks abounded for long-service awards. In the current world, long-service awards are rarer since loyalty to and by one company or organization is almost a forgotten thing. Even in the sporting field change is all-pervasive. We have had the English soccer team coached and managed by a Swede; and Welsh and Italian rugby teams have been coached and managed by New Zealanders. More nationalities are represented in the English soccer premiership than there are teams in the league.

And yet ... there is an inbuilt paradox here. Organizations need to perform, to grow and nurture talent *and* operate as a collection of individuals at the same time. They need to act as a global unit, corporately, and at the same time have entrepreneurial individual leaders furthering their own careers within that organization. The organization wants to have its cake and eat it, while the individual slices might get eaten willingly by another organization.

Rosabeth Moss Kanter wrote in her book *When Giants Learn to Dance* that 'when companies encourage their managers to become more professional and more entrepreneurial, they are also encouraging them to develop their own judgement about what the company needs'. In the past, an individual may have put loyalty to the company first, the team second and their professional skills third. The emphasis has reversed and organizations are having to recognize this. Individual growth and development benefits the individual and, through him, the organization. It is the organization's job to harness the talents and energies of its people. The coach's job is to build them up and bring them to bear fruit.

The coach can play a central position between organizational and individual need, and be able to work actively with the individual across this boundary, combining both the corporate agenda and the personal agenda. An illustration might help.

A chief executive of an asset management company had just been promoted from a group of peers into that position and was now responsible to the chair based in the USA. It was a worldwide activity with many billions of pounds' worth of assets under management. The organizational agenda was clear:

- to make a success of the appointment in the first year and to ensure his effectiveness in retaining the services of key people in the operation; and
- to blend together a new team to meet the organization's three critical objectives of performance, performance, performance!

The individual's personal agenda was multi-hatted:

- to raise his own awareness of what skills and qualities he was bringing into the role;
- to achieve a satisfactory work/life balance as he absorbed himself into the new role, while delivering the organization's agenda effectively; and
- to find time to prepare himself for non-executive roles in three to five years' time by raising his profile in the market, amongst other things, and to be able to devote time to improve his piano playing – finding time to gain more time for other things!

As the coaching progressed and moved through the organization and personal agendas, it was augmented by a third agenda – the 'personal at work'. What we mean by 'personal at work' are those things which affect the work agenda but are private to the individual in the workplace, e.g. lacking confidence in giving presentations to large groups or feeling a need to be more inspirational in their leadership. What concerned him was that his predecessor (whom he had served under and who had retired) had used a very autocratic style. The client knew his own style was more consensual and believed that he had no option but to change to become more autocratic. This led to discussions about being autocratic versus being authoritative in style and thus becoming authentic to himself and being authoritative. He was relieved: he realized he could have a natural authority; he didn't have to 'change' to be autocratic as he had expected! In talking about coaching, this CEO said:

> 'As team leader, the CEO will come to appreciate that the best teams combine different skill sets. For starters, therefore, he needs to know

his own skill set and how he will add value to the enterprise. Once he does, his feeling of self-worth is likely to grow and his effectiveness also ... At a time of possible isolation, it is critical for a CEO to have someone who is sympathetic, challenging when appropriate and independent.'

Straddling this 'personal at work' boundary between organization and individual is an important reason for the growth in business coaching. Charles Handy has often said that what gets onto a boardroom agenda (profit margins, sales, office moves, acquisitions, etc.) is not what really makes the boardroom more or less effective (fear, envy, greed, rivalry and competition between board members). It is these issues that should be on the agenda.

Changing demands and expectations on leaders

Leaders are experiencing a double whammy: first, at any one point in time, there appears to be not enough time to do all the things that need to be done; second, there are not enough sequences of time to build up the in-depth experience that used to be possible.

The demands and expectations placed upon leaders today are legion. In a global email-ridden and internet-based environment, the difficulty of leading and managing a virtual team provides almost insuperable problems for some leaders. Even if there is time allocated to attend a business school course or a top management programme, there is limited real-time opportunity to put the learning into practice in the workplace. If children need time to do homework and practice what they are taught when they are in full-time learning, then why should we expect it to be easier for an executive? It is too glib to say that all of us should adopt a universal and abiding approach to 'learning while we do', but our friendly TINA is ever present – Time Is Not Available!

Following the terrorist bombs in New York in 2001, we held a forum in London with senior executive clients on the theme of 'Leadership in Uncertain Times'. Their reflections were that:

- the motivation to succeed and aim for the top has changed;
- younger people are more amenable to portfolio careers and recent events have only accelerated this;
- more leadership is required and less leadership is available;
- a different kind of leadership is required for virtual teams;
- if people are making life changes and moving on, then leading and managing those who are left takes on a new significance; and

- there is an even greater requirement for situational leadership – different styles which can be used with agility in different situations – but there is a need to build respect for leaders in normal times in order to have respect for them when they act differently.

The independent sounding board or coach in these scenarios provides a focussed, relevant and timely way for individuals to consider and work out appropriate action.

The continued rise of compliance and governance rules for organizations of all shapes and sizes worldwide is evident to all. While these rules are in place to put controls on the minority, they affect the majority. Business decisions demand judgement, and no amount of governance can provide for this if judgement is absent. Judgement takes time to acquire and is a complex combination of experience, intellect, intuition and insight as well as sensitivity.

An organization with around 1300 outlets within the UK and Ireland faces a perennial challenge not uncommon in its retail sector. The energy and enthusiasm of executive youth is not necessarily matched by a breadth of experience. Changing jobs frequently helps build up experience, but one individual who got to the CEO role in the UK found that, with a number of acquisitions, the change agenda was broader than he had ever experienced. His judgement was being tested in areas of brand management, IT platform expansion and focus and culture change, as well as by keeping the sales up and his team focused on results. Headlines in the press and the consequent PR demands on his time added to the picture.

One investment bank refers to 'battlefield promotions' within its organization. Youthful individuals step up to newly vacated or created leadership positions in an ever-expanding industry in financial services. How do you give people the 'broad shoulders' and judgement necessary to handle these leadership roles? Confidence and willingness is there in abundance, as may be the interpersonal skills. But as Sir Christopher Walford told Robin after 35 years in the legal profession:

There is a great danger of losing wisdom, maturity and experience [as the over 50s retire early or are made redundant] ... you cannot instil into a 25-year-old the practical experience that has been built up over 20 years ... you can't grasp overnight the knowledge of different markets and different trading conditions.'

Coaching can help in this acquisition of 'broad shoulders' by allowing a focused period of time to reflect on what a leader does and thinks, which is where wisdom and learning begins. For the busy business leader, a period of reflection is the beginning of business wisdom.

The relevance of strategic leadership frameworks for coaching

New leadership frameworks compiling sets of values and competences have reinforced the importance of coaching as part of strategic leadership development, where organizations are looking at their top people in the context of the whole future of the enterprise. This is what Alistair Mant, in his book *Intelligent Leadership*, referred to as the difference between 'bike thinking' and 'frog thinking'. A bike you can take apart, taking off the chain, wheels, handlebars, pedals and frame, etc. then put it together again, so that it can still be a bicycle. If you take bits off a frog, there comes a time when it ceases to be a frog, however much you might try to sew bits back on: it is a system. There are parts of organizations that are definitely 'bike-ish' and parts that are definitely 'frog-ish'. It is one thing to tinker with the organization chart (bike-ish) and another to seriously look at the organization culture, processes and systems (frog-ish). Leadership development and coaching fall into the latter category and cannot be seen in isolation.

For example, two companies in totally different markets show a similar approach to setting the framework for coaching to take place.

- **Company A** – an industrial concern operating worldwide has developed a set of leadership competencies that provide a common language for individual executives to use. The aim is to increase the strength of the pool of talent as well as the options for succession planning. The whole framework is built around the strategy for the business and the people strategy is integral to that.
- **Company B** – is in the financial services market, operating worldwide, and is again gearing its whole approach to developing pools of talent at various levels from graduate to executive.

Key components and considerations for coaching in both of these companies are:

- *Developing a common leadership language* – this helps to keep everybody in the organization in the same book (if not necessarily on the same page at any one time!).
- *Keeping a business focus* – individuals need to learn how to lead and manage their own businesses as well as appreciate and understand the management and leadership of all business lines.
- *Cultural awareness* – where is the business base coming from in two, five or ten years' time? People need to be prepared for that business market

today – age, ethnicity, gender, country culture, diverse skills and qualities, etc.

- *Learning styles* – how do you help senior executive 'experts' shift to also become 'learners' when big egos are at stake?
- *Accountability* – how can leaders be accountable:
  - to their role in their organization?
  - to their peers?
  - to other staff as a role model?
- *Personal Development Plans* – senior executives may not consider it necessary to have these since they are 'for others'! How can the concept be accepted, even if not using the term 'Personal Development Plan'? How can you get to the core issues and points in the Personal Development Plan?

The essential question with which organizations are having to grapple is: 'How do you make leaders more able to leave the organization but also more likely to stay?'

Robin recalls the leadership demonstrated by a fellow corporate finance partner in his accounting firm. To get a return from the investment in a training contract, the aim was to ensure those who qualified stayed at least a further two or three years. At the point of qualification the head hunters were very active. One qualified accountant resigned, but was encouraged by the partner to see three other banks and then come back to compare offerings – he stayed a further three years!

While there is increasing use (and sometimes misuse) of psychological and other assessment tools to discover the abilities and suitabilities of leaders, there is an increasing need to apply the 'so what next?' test to all the data accumulated. A chief executive might say, 'We now know via our due diligence that we have two world-class, two industry-class, ten average and two below-average leaders in the organization we are acquiring so ... how do we retain the top four? How do we develop the ten? What do we do with this data?'

Focused coaching for accelerated development can be one part of the answer. The good coach will have an unchanging belief that there is more to people than meets the eye – that what you see even in a good performance in the arts or business world has still greater potential within it. It is a highly unusual parent who thinks that his or her child cannot develop further. Maybe it is because parents want the best so badly that they disregard the true ability level in the arena they are interested in, yet if they step back and look at other qualities their youngster possesses and enable that potential to be released differently, then who knows what is possible!

To get the most out of a climbing plant you need some kind of support or trellis. To get the most out of people, especially those with high potential, you need a structural framework. This may be an organizational structure, it may be a framework of beliefs or values that are held strongly, or it may be a framework of leadership development. Ideally it will be a combination of all of these elements and any other frameworks that are clearly articulated, collectively understood and fit culturally. Individuals need reference points.

Each person in an organization has a part to play. The chief executive can't function without the security guard and the receptionist; the marketing assistant needs direction from his director; the senior executive or high potential individual, to fulfil their potential, needs access to a coach. They *all* need the person or persons behind the machine that provides coffee! There is a network of dependent and interdependent relationships but this can only thrive where there is:

- mutual respect – a recognition of ability, contribution and role; and
- mutuality of service – both a need to lead and direct *and* to encourage and support.

Creating the right environment for effective leadership development

What can organizations do to create this 'emergent leadership' environment of mutual respect and mutuality of service? Leaders have to operate nationally and globally and switch flexibly between the two. They need to be conscious of the many local, national and international environments and the context in which they work. When organizations and their leaders work in these overlapping arenas, there are three things they can do and where coaching can play a part. Firstly, they can state clearly their role in their 'corporate social' community: they should be seen to be concerned just as much as they are concerned to be seen. Secondly, they can create a communicating organization where the inhibitions of hierarchy have been removed, with linkages and networks fostered to allow potential to flourish. Thirdly they can provide a learning environment and a coaching culture – one where self-reliance is encouraged and interdependence is nurtured at one and the same time. Then and only then can coaching achieve its fullest impact.

Chapter 4:

What Makes a Good Coach?

This chapter looks at what makes a good coach focusing in particular on:
- the perspectives of those commissioning coaching;
- the focus on 'outwardness' or outward-looking in coaching engagements;
- where the coach starts;
- the nature of learning conversations;
- the three 'Es' of 'Encourage', 'Experience' and 'Enlighten';
- confidentiality and ethics;
- sound supervision;
- the skills and competences a coach uses;
- coaching qualifications and accreditation;
- thought leadership; and
- the value of a dynamic coaching relationship changing over time.

There is a strong theme of ensuring high quality running through each of these strands. The good coach will set and maintain high standards of professionalism, keep up to date and have a wide range of competences.

Hazel, a buyer of coaching in a national organization, describes her approach to recruitment of coaches as, 'I'm looking for coaches with a wide range of skills, models, scenarios and strategies. I need coaches who are going to be challenging and can bring a hard-nosed push towards goals.'

Each coach will bring a different approach to his or her work. There is no such thing as a neutral question since every good coach will have an aim or purpose behind asking the question in the first place.

So what makes a good coach? Coaches will bring their personalities and backgrounds to bear on the situations their clients present. Some coaches will have extensive, senior-level business experience and be familiar with the boardroom on a personal level; others will have a deep psychological understanding and expertise which informs their work. Many will have both of these.

A good coach needs to be effective in understanding:

- the role and dynamics of the organization;
- the person and personality of the client;
- the situation the client is in;
- the stage of learning the client is at; and
- the process of the client relationship.

What differentiates the best coaching is this clarity of understanding of both the organization and the individual.

Is the client dependent on relationships for who they are? Do they get their identity from the institution they represent ('I am a member of X group' or 'I am a lawyer!')? Is the client fully self-aware and able to look objectively as an outsider at him or herself as an individual? A person could remain dependent on a group for their identity for the bulk of their earthly life. Through questioning, an effective coach will encourage an individual to greater self-awareness using a range of ideas and models as a backdrop.

Perspectives of those commissioning coaching

We asked a number of users of coaches to identify what they looked for in coaches: what qualities and attitudes and orientations make for a good coach.

> 'They must have a good level of insight into themselves as to their own strengths and weaknesses. The coach must be clear what is their 'A' game and have an intuitive feeling for our business. They must bring a range of tools in their toolkit and know when to use them. They must not be a one-track wonder. They need to be skilled artisans taking their development seriously and seeing coaching as a profession.'
>
> Noel Hadden

> 'Flexibility of approach is important: different coachees need different coaching styles. There must be clear professional training and a strong track record. There need to be people saying that the coach has made a real difference. Strong personal reputation is vital. The coach must be able to listen, reflect and play back focusing on the coachee's agenda and not their own personal agenda. The coach must be clear that coaching

is not welfare counselling: it must impact on the performance of the organization.'

Hilary Douglas

'High-quality skills of questioning and listening are basic. There must be enough understanding about the organization to understand where people are coming from and to fully appreciate the value set. There needs to be enough knowledge of the environment to help somebody through their journey and then the application of tough coaching skills.'

Rob Edwards

'A lot of experience and training is needed to be a good coach. Competence is a prerequisite. Coaches must make a real difference to the performance of the organization. Coaches must ensure that the client uses the opportunity to go to a deeper level.'

Jill King

'I look for breadth of experience in terms of the coach's own work and the people they work with. The mindset must be the coach wanting the best for the individual and the organization and linking the two together. There needs to be good-quality experience of coaching. Psychometrics and specific coaching qualifications are not high on my list of priorities.'

John Bailey

'Coaches should be able to evaluate without being judgemental. They must be able to evaluate the impact of their approach. I am not in favour of coaching without content. A good coach must be able to know when to offer steers. They must be able to sift through conflicting information and be able to see the wood for the trees. They need good professional training and have a genuine desire to support people.'

Philippa Charles

These comments cover coaches having insight into themselves, a range of tools in their toolkit, flexibility, listening skills, experience, challenge, goal orientation, questioning skills, the ability to go 'deep', wanting the best for the individual and the organization, as well as the ability to work within the business context.

All of these qualities of a good coach emanate from perspectives in the above quotes. Three areas we believe to be crucial are:

- being grounded and having deep self-awareness;

- not seeking to achieve one's own ambitions through others; and
- holding unconditional positive regard for the client.

It is this latter quality of '*unconditional* positive regard' which means the coach can orient towards selflessness while being 'self-aware' or possessing 'outwardness'.

Outwardness

It is very easy for a coach to fall into being 'inward looking'. The coach has their own learning to do and tools to develop for use in the coaching process and here comes a client 'on whom I can practise!' When talking with HR Directors, Learning and Development Department Heads and Talent Managers who are the 'gate keepers' for coaching initiatives in organizations, we are often asked: 'What's your model for coaching?' At one level, the answer could be very simplistic and easy to define. We might use the GROW (Goal, Reality, Options, Way forward) model in working through a session with a client. We might work with Transactional Analysis and look for responses that are adult to adult, or for unexpected responses that are adult to 'adopted child'. We might work with Neuro-Linguistic Programming, Cognitive Behavioural Therapy, or solution-based approaches (these are all discussed in Chapter 9).

When answering the 'model' question in this way, it is as though it is assumed we have an agenda which we are going to use with any client, come what may, or else we can work only with certain clients for whom this particular approach is relevant. Coaching is often not so ordered. Myles Downey in his book *Effective Coaching* (p34) refers to the role of the coach as encouraging the client to think and not to do the thinking for them:

> '*The need is to stay on their agenda and to follow their interest. There is a need to expand (what's going on in the situation? What else? What else? ...) and then to focus (so which element would you wish to concentrate on? Which is most interesting to you?)*'

This he calls the Model T and this is a model of *how* to ask questions rather than *what* questions to ask. The coach has to be adaptable and flexible to be able to use what is appropriate.

At another level however the answer to 'What's your model for coaching?' lies in the coaching engagement itself. If a coach is going to work with a client, then the coach has to get onto the person's agenda. What is it that the individual needs and wants to work on, and can the coach help in any way? The individual client may have chosen to have coaching for themselves and have a clear agenda. If the coach can provide help then there is a purpose to the relationship and the client will drive it. It may well be that the individual's agenda will be helped by the use of several different 'models' which the coach has in their repertoire – these models, however, are not the agenda.

If the coach has this 'outwardness' and can learn to stay on the client's agenda, then the coaching relationship will be balanced and is likely to be effective.

Where does the coach start?

A good coach gets to the heart of the agenda very quickly by using effective questioning and being 'with the client' in their situation at the same time as being objectively distant from the client. Getting the objectives clear for coaching is paramount. (In Chapter 5, we look more closely at objective setting.)

Helping an individual address the right questions is central to good coaching. We struggle to do this for ourselves. Robin vividly remembers a time when he tried to start his automatic car without success. Frantic to get somewhere on time, he turned and turned the key. He was about to call out the garage and to identify his problem as 'the car won't start'. The last thing he wanted to do was to go through a litany of questions with the garage receptionist about where he lived, who he was, type of car, how old it is, etc; he just wanted the problem fixed! He then looked down and realised the gear stick was in D for Drive *not* P for Park. This was a powerful picture for Robin about addressing the right question! An independent coach who is effective will get to the 'key' questions immediately.

Time is a precious commodity and problems get in the way all the time. In Tom's case overleaf, as a new Finance Director, he couldn't see a way through initially so he buried himself in his new role by continuing in his 'old' ways. The problem was he was still mentally in his old role and the coach had to enter into his world. It is a coach's 'outwardness' that is the starting point for any effective coach.

Tom: an illustration

We now pull these strands together in a brief illustration of how questioning techniques in coaching can operate on several levels and it is as though the coach is having 'learning conversations with a client'.

'I want to start the coaching but it's not the right time yet – I've got too much on at the moment.' This was Tom, a newly appointed Finance Director in the Executive Team of an industrial company, in a telephone conversation with his coach. His organization had agreed that coaching should happen: the CEO and HR Director had briefed the coach and asked him to phone Tom for a chemistry meeting. The background noise suggested almost bedlam in the workplace. As he seemed so busy, the coach went to see Tom in his office once they had managed to get a date in the diary (very early in the morning).

The coach's reaction? 'This will be hard work!' Tom ended up coming to the coach's office for meetings 'because he was supposed to'. Since Tom tended to live on his wits, the first session's objective was all about time management and organization, starting with the question 'How many meetings do you call and how many meetings are you called for?' The question stumped him for a moment but it led into an important discussion about roles.

Tom had no idea of what his new role as FD was and what value it would add to the organization, because in his new office he was no longer 'at his desk at the beck and call of his team'. His inclination was to be heavily involved on the financial accounting side, and he loved it when someone was away so he could be back in role talking to the financial accountants in the operation division, doing budgets, monthly spreadsheets and overall consolidated summaries for the Executive Team. Tom needed to agree his role with the CEO and to identify indicators about what would constitute success in the role.

Then there was the question of delegation. Tom tended to distance himself and didn't like to say 'no' to any request. He would just get on and do it, even if it was difficult. His job as FD now required him to be away in continental Europe three days per week, so he had to learn to delegate. The coach made an analysis with him of the qualities of people now reporting to him across Treasury, Tax, Operational Accounting and Shared Services.

Tom was dealing with issues he had not come across before. In his first six months, he got dumped upon and involved in negotiations with a French company about an alliance, and he seemed to handle it quite well. The coach talked with him about moving into a new arena and what that meant in terms of the old reality and new reality, the old self and the new self, what he had managed and led and the way he might want to manage and lead in the future.

Tom came across the Corporate Development Director doing a deal in Germany, which was running parallel with his own efforts in Germany. He was furious and wanted to know how to handle this. How could he cope with emerging relationships with people in Germany and with those of his team? He now had to learn to manage 'upwards' in the organization, work with peers and compete for the time of the CEO and make full use of it when he got it. Gone were the days of the one-on-one relationship he had had with his boss, the Fed, when he was the Financial Controller. Tom was now one of several directors competing for the time of the CEO, and he needed different influencing skills.

By this time, Tom was seeing the sessions as an opportunity to review and to ask: 'What did I learn from that?'. He began to use the coaching services in a different way. Tom had to give a talk on 'The Future of the Finance Scene in Europe' and his coach acted as an independent but questioning Non-Executive Director, operating as a sounding board. The coach was a disinterested outsider interested in his success.

As they worked together, the relationship between coach and individual had changed in two ways.

- The FD would have said at the beginning that he needed to 'learn management techniques'; now he would see it as enabling him to examine what he is doing and then to plan forward.
- The initial aim and objective had changed. The client had moved from management techniques (time management/delegation) to defining a strategic view of the marketplace.

Learning conversations

There are many ways of approaching the relationship between coach and client. One approach is to see the relationship as a sequence of learning conversations.

At the *basic level* $L(0)$ this is to do with the 'what' of the client's job. In Tom's case, this was the elements in the new role of being Finance Director. Essentially this is about problem solving together.

A managing partner of a law firm wanted to initiate changes in her organization. The previous incumbent had adopted a very authoritarian style, dictating where the firm should go and what it should do and the way it needed to do it. The incoming managing partner felt the groundswell amongst many partners that an 'authoritative' but more 'consensual' style would be acceptable. Several key commercial indicators were in need of revamp, profitability needed to be given focus and not just revenue, and there needed to be greater cross-selling across the firm. Clients were seeking solutions across corporate, employment, litigation, property and intellectual property departments; clients needed to be account-managed and a whole new customer relationship management structure put in place.

The coach and the managing partner worked on this problem together at the level of what needed to be done. The particular tool that was helpful came from John Kotter's book *Leading Change*, and they both went through the framework of eight steps in effective change programmes. Issues facing the managing partner were addressed, such as her relationships with other partners as well as the implications of each element of the process for her and for others. This coaching relationship stayed at L(O) for about six months.

At the next level L(1) the conversation between coach and client will move to the 'how' in that the client begins to address the thinking about how she does her job. In Tom's case this was all the delegation and ways of managing in his new role as FD.

A director in a real estate advisory organization was going through a major change process. Another framework similar to the 'John Kotter process' had been used at the problem-solving L(O) stage by the coach. The mechanics and logistics of the change agenda were well in hand. The key issue emerging, however, was to do with the personalities of the key people involved in and affected by the change. The coach realized he could not just apply the process mechanically. This fitted with the individual's highly logical and analytical approach, but he began to realize that he was not engaging people in a way which was helpful: he had to take action to engage people effectively. It was then the client realized that the style he was using to manage change was so important. The coach worked with him on this need for flexibility and practised with him in role-plays some of the different styles he could adopt.

At the advanced level (2) the client is concerned about learning to learn. The conversation turns to thinking about how the client thinks about doing her job. In the case of the director in the real estate advisory firm, it is when he began to ask questions like: 'What are the occasions when I begin to think about how I do my job? What are the ways in which I can create those occasions for review and reflection?' In Tom's case, he began to use the coaching sessions to ask: 'What did I learn from that?'

An investment banker who organizes hundreds of technologists on various IT projects around the world has developed the habit of 'creating white spaces'. He knows that, when a big report comes in, he needs to have a clear three hours in his diary to think about the implications before he calls in his team to begin to even get their views. He asks his PA to ensure his diary is cleared for that purpose. Coaching at this level is about 90% inspiration, 10% perspiration and not the other way round. The character in Gilbert and Sullivan's *Gondoliers* conveyed this notion of L(2) when he said:

'In a contemplative fashion,
And a tranquil frame of mind,
Free from every kind of passion,
Some solution let us find.
Let us grasp the situation
Solve the complicated plot –
Quiet, calm deliberation
Disentangles every knot.'

The three 'E's

Another way of looking at where the coach can start with a client is to see the relationship as a continuance of a client's life. Many clients will start at the point of wanting to consider their future and where their career is heading. What will they do in the last few years before retirement? How can they gain a different work/life balance? How can they develop greater impact and gravitas?

All of us have a past, a present and a future and the coaching relationship can start at any point where the client feels it should. Table 4.1 shows a simple framework for this idea.

The 3 'E's of 'Encourage', 'Experience' and 'Enlighten' take us into the next section about what a coach brings to each meeting with a client in order to be effective. If the start is in the past, then the coach will encourage hindsight to look back at the strengths of the client and also where there are 'understrengths' – points in their life when a skill was used and enjoyed but has become almost dormant and needs to be revived.

Where the start of the engagement is in the present, then the client can experience insights into what is happening in the job right now. The coach may well move to working in the moment in each session with the client. Jim is a director in a private bank who expressed deep dissatisfaction with his CEO, who had criticized him over the way he had presented a report to the management team. He had also told his coach in a previous session that

Past	Hindsight	Encourage – do well what you can do
Present	Insight	Experience – gain learning 'in the moment'
Future	Foresight	Enlighten – push into new comfort zones

Table. 4.1 A simple framework for starting a coaching relationship

he was entirely open to criticism and wanted to learn. The coach was able to 'use the moment' in reflecting back his defensiveness and lack of openness to criticism in the way he talked about his CEO. This insight enabled him to reflect on his experience in the session and to plan a course of action.

Where the start of the engagement is in the future, then foresight can be used to help the client become enlightened on what may be possible – there is a new opportunity to push into a new comfort zone. The Finance Director earlier in the chapter had taken on a new role and, working with him on moving into a new arena, the coach was able to 'push the boundaries'.

Confidentiality and ethics

Unless a client understands that he or she can talk freely and openly in a coaching relationship, then coaching will be ineffective. Confidentiality is critical to such a trusting situation.

Individual clients may want to raise questions such as:

- Will the agenda I have agreed with you, my coach, be made available to my organization?
- With whom will you (the coach) discuss matters raised in our sessions?
- Do you, the coach, know anything about me that I don't know, having talked to my organization?
- Can I see a copy of the coaching notes you write?
- Where will those notes be filed and who will have access?

Sponsoring organizations might be asking:

- Can you, the coach, give me a progress report on how the coaching is going?
- We have an on-line time schedule for updating progress in all our executive coaching which we will expect you to complete both qualitatively and quantitatively. Will you do so as X's coach?
- What will you do as X's coach if you discover that X needs access to expertise that you, the coach, do not possess?

A coach must have clear professional guidelines and guidance in order to address these effectively. All of these questions raise not only the question of confidentiality but also the ethical boundaries surrounding the coaching relationship. At the outset therefore it is essential that coach, client and sponsor are all clear on the 'contractual' arrangements.

Best practice indicates that all coaching relationships need to have an agreed set of arrangements between coach, client and sponsor setting out the expectations for the coaching, e.g.:

- The objectives
- All matters discussed between client and coach are confidential to that relationship unless the client determines otherwise.
- The coach will seek the client's agreement to record notes of their meetings.
- Discussions with the client may be referred to by the coach in discussions with their professional supervisor.

Many matters such as those above fall into the area of the Code of Ethics by which a coach operates and to which he or she will subscribe. One such code is that provided by the European Mentoring and Coaching Council which is available on its website at www.emccouncil.org.

Sound supervision

A key factor in ensuring high-quality coaching is rigorous professional supervision. This must not be skimped. Quality professional supervision is crucial for any good coach to be really effective. Supervision allows the coach to have a formal process of structured reflection with a trained supervisor about the quality of their coaching and how they are developing as a coach.

Early in 2007, The Chartered Institute of Personnel and Development published an excellent guide, *Coaching Supervision: Maximising the potential of coaching.* It stated how few coaches are receiving this valuable support:

'While 86% of coaches responding to our survey believe that coaches should have coaching supervision, only 44% actually do so ... The gap is even greater for those who organize coaching services. In all, 88% say they believe coaches should have supervision, but only 23% report that they provide it'.

Of those coaches who have received supervision, less than half had received it for more than two years.

It is critical that standards are applied to this growing profession of coaching. Supervision is challenging for the coach and prevents the coach from getting too 'close' to the client. The coach needs to retain as objective a stance as possible.

An effective coach enables a client to grow, make choices, develop as a leader and become the best person they can be both now and in the future.

Behind the scenes of that coach/client relationship, it is essential that there is a supervisor working with the coach to enable that coach to:

- maintain and enhance the quality of their coaching and undertake appropriate work with clients (*qualitative*);
- address the skills, understanding and capabilities needed to work with clients (*developmental*); and
- understand their own emotions and involvement with their clients to ensure that their work is as objective as possible (*resourcing*).

The descriptions in brackets above are the definitions of the three main functions of effective coaching supervision set out by Hawkins & Smith (2006) in their Open University Press publication *Coaching, mentoring and organizational consultancy: supervision and development.*

A supervisor could be an experienced coach, a psychotherapist or a psychologist but, whatever their background, they will be trained in supervision skills and techniques. Such a supervisor is an essential part of a coach's experience and will enhance the process of coaching.

Many of the ethical pitfalls referred to above can be discussed and avoided through the process of supervision. A supervisor will enable the coach to be far more self-aware and will be prepared to take risks with feedback by holding up a mirror to the coach so they can see themselves in a different light. Supervision can be about helping coaches to reframe situations they are finding themselves in with their clients, e.g. how to disentangle the client's agenda from the client's cultural/company agenda and from the coach's own emotional agenda. There are many dimensions to consider.

When buying coaching, the purchaser should satisfy itself that the coaching organization has effective supervision arrangements. Questions that should be asked by the purchaser of any prospective coach include the following.

- Are you receiving coaching supervision?
- What training has your supervisor undertaken to be able to supervise?
- What have been your learning experiences through supervision?
- Do all your clients get 'covered' by supervision of your coaches?
- How regularly does supervision take place? Is it one-to-one or as a group of coaches?
- How has supervision made a difference to you as a coach?

Quality providers of coaching will be distinguished by their use of an approach to supervision. They will readily acknowledge that the quality of supervision is an essential input to the quality of coaching.

What skills and competences does a coach use?

The quote from a buyer of coaching at the beginning of this chapter emphasized the need for a coach to have a 'wide range of skills, models, scenarios and strategies'. Recent literature often refers to the 'eclectic model' of coaching (Hardingham (2006)/Megginson & Clutterbuck (2005)). We prefer to use the word 'integrated' to describe this aspect of a coach's competence.

We do not have one particular model that we, as coaches, 'apply' to a client. The good coach will have a range of learning, approaches and techniques that they have acquired and continue to acquire. When a client has a particular challenge, a good coach draws upon the approaches that are most appropriate for the client at that point in time.

In any sphere of learning there is an ideal progression through:

(a) knowing nothing (unconscious incompetence); and
(b) knowing that there is lots I do not know (conscious incompetence);
(c) knowing things very well (conscious competence); to
(d) knowing them so well that it is natural, part of me or 'integrated' (unconscious competence).

The compilation of knowledge in (a), (b) and (c) ensures awareness of the 'range' of material available to a coach. The 'integration' of all this material within the coach at (d) is the key to effective coaching.

The coach needs to have an approach to coaching that brings into play a wide variety of tools and techniques, which can be distilled and sieved for the client's benefit, for example:

- management theories;
- theories about personal development; and
- understanding of psychological models and approaches.

There will be many approaches in the toolkit of the effective coach. The client will have a particular objective to achieve and the coach will be able to help in using a model or tool or technique appropriately and in context.

The coach will be giving the client unconditional, positive regard and will be absolutely focused on the client and the situation the client is in. The good business coach will operate partly as a management consultant, partly as a mentor, partly as a counsellor and partly as a developer of people. In whatever 'role' the coach operates, they will operate in a natural, integrated way. The coach will be 'present' with the client and know intuitively what is the right thing to ask or do. That intuition will have been and is being fed by a 'wide range of skills, models, scenarios and strategies'.

The model of competences we use currently is shown in Fig.4.1.

The competencies can be summarized as follows, since the effectiveness of the coach lies in the range as well as the depth of competence.

- *Business*: This is the knowledge and understanding of business princi-ples, processes, challenges and developments. It will demand a body of experience of management theory, organization dynamics and work practices and an awareness of the different techniques used in the rel-evant business area.
- *Consultancy*: The ability to interpret and analyse issues as well as develop ideas and facilitate change underlies this area of competence.
- *Developer of People*: This is the desire and ability to enable people to learn and develop. It involves understanding the way people grow and the stages of transition across lives and careers together with understanding of the learning cycle and the different approaches that can be adopted in learning.
- *Interpersonal*: This embraces the qualities of active listening and those aspects which enable the coach to respect all people and relate effectively with different types of people. It includes the coach using him or herself as an instrument so that they use their own reactions as indicative of the reactions of others. It means bringing a cross-cultural understanding to it. It is about a personal presence that inspires the best in others.

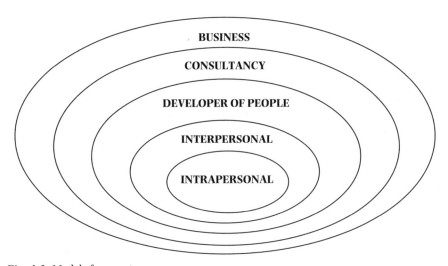

Fig. 4.1 Model of competences

- *Intrapersonal*: At the core of a coach's competence are an enhanced self-awareness and an appreciation of self-control and self-worth. It is about reading and understanding one's own emotions and their impact. It is about the ability to be relaxed and open with others and the capacity to express self-confidence, joy and humility.

Coaching qualifications and accreditation

How do you obtain these skills and competences? How does the purchaser know which coach is 'qualified' and which coach isn't 'qualified'? There is intense interest in the notion of coaches being 'accredited' to be able to undertake work with clients.

Many schools and training providers have set up courses and programmes to train coaches. The EMCC (European Mentoring and Coaching Council) has sought to establish 'quality marks' for these providers via its EMCC Quality Award scheme throughout Europe (more about this features in Chapter 13 (page 204), under the heading *International Consistency of Standards*

Individual coaches have to demonstrate that they have the credibility, body of knowledge, professional orientation (ethically and practically) and understanding to be able to undertake the work of a business coach. The fact that coaches have been on a two-week, two-month or even two-year course does not mean they are good coaches. It does mean that they have started on the process of learning about themselves as a coach and what exactly they are doing when they coach in any given situation.

A business coach might have qualifications to administer psychometric instruments, a diploma/advanced diploma/Masters in executive coaching, a knowledge of psychological theories and have attended a programme about Gestalt Psychology – all of these and more are part and parcel of the 'integrated' approach to coaching to which we subscribe and which we describe elsewhere in this book.

Above all, however, for a business coach there has to be some acknowledgement of prior learning obtained from many years of experience as a business executive, whether in the public or private sector or both. The twin tracks of being acknowledged as an individual with senior business executive experience and being accredited as an expert coach are essential foundations for the good business coach.

Quality of coaching results from both initial qualification and continuous professional development. A good coaching organization will have a rigorous programme of professional development enabling coaches to keep up to date with the latest business and coaching good practice.

Thought leadership

We believe that good coaches will be continually pressing the boundaries of understanding. They will be operating at the cutting edge of developing good practice; hence our belief in the importance of participating in seminars and dialogues with businesses and academics. Our objective is to share our experience through articles and books so the quality of what we do is raised. We believe that good coaches will be playing their part in developing and publicizing best practice. This is a further input to enhancing coaching quality.

A dynamic coaching relationship changing over time

There is a school of thought that says coaching must have clear short-term objectives and, once the objectives are achieved, the coaching stops. This is a very valid approach in many circumstances. There is another school that looks at coaching as a sequence of changing objectives, because the client is dynamic and the client's situation is dynamic. This can lead to coaching relationships existing over longer periods of time, going through distinct phases.

It is our experience that many senior people will benefit from coaching with the same coach over long periods. We both work with clients where we are moving into the second, third and in one case fifth year of coaching. Why is this? There are at least four areas of change that operate where the strength of engagement built up over a period between coach and client can be invaluable in working through new challenges.

- **Organizational change** – the client will attain different and frequently bigger, new roles as an organization acquires, merges, demerges, expands in markets, etc., leading to restructurings.
- **Market change** – some individuals and sectors are continuously renewing and refreshing their products and services. Working with someone who has high potential means working with them through many new dimensions, culturally, economically and in scope of their budgetary activity.
- **Personal change** – individual client circumstances change from, for example, being able to travel extensively to needing to be more domestic; or from sensing that their career is on track with one company to being off track when it is taken over. The long-term agenda may keep changing as a result.

- **Agenda change** – this is the shift from the longer-term agenda which gets more and more deferred because (legitimate) short-term agenda items become dominant.

The purchaser of a new car moves from running the car in through to international driving, through its first crash, through to MOTs being necessary after three years. In the same way, a client's career demands different coaching needs, and the relationship can continue very fruitfully provided there is regular re-evaluation and revision of objectives.

Nick Brown, the Chief Executive of SERCO Integrated Transport, has had the same coach for 15 years. He talks of a relationship that has gone in distinct phases: sometimes it has been meeting once every six weeks, while on other occasions it has been a phone call every three months. He says the key requirement is that the client continues to feel there is 'meat in the relationship' and that the coach can quickly understand 'where you are on the pitch'. The long-term relationship provides a strong mutual understanding, but the relationship must not be so close that objectivity is diminished.

Conclusion

We have sought to identify what makes an effective coach. Being client focused and client centred is at the heart of effective engagement. The use of different skills and techniques will be dictated by the client's agenda. The coach will need to undergo supervision to ensure that she is maintaining independence and professionalism in the coaching process. This is addressed in our next chapter, *What a client gets out of engaging with coaching*.

Chapter 5:

What a Client Gets out of Engaging with Coaching

This chapter addresses the following themes:
- what coaching can do for an individual, covering business issues, clarity of role, personal awareness and interpersonal skills;
- what the experience of being coached is like, covering standing back to reflect, understanding perceptions, facing up to key issues, increasing personal impact, improving communications and learning about yourself;
- what happens in a coaching discussion;
- coaching as dynamic conversation;
- the importance of clarity of objectives;
- clarity of feedback;
- the effective matching of coach and client; and
- the impact of coaching across an individual's life.

Success comes when there is a strong commitment of coach, client and sponsoring organization to a high quality of input and the dynamic nature of the engagement.

What can coaching do for an individual?

In early 2006, an independent survey was conducted of 80 individuals who are coached by members of the Partnership of which we are members. Individuals were asked about the objectives for the coaching and its outcomes. The main types of objectives were as follows:

- *business issues*: strategic priorities, business planning, major projects;
- *clarity of role*: transitional coaching into a new role, career development and preparation for subsequent roles;

- *personal awareness*: impact, leadership style, confidence, self-belief and assertiveness; and
- *interpersonal skills*: influencing skills, stakeholder management and team management and development.

Some of the key outcomes reported by individuals were about professional development: they understood cultural issues within the organization better, had a bigger impact within the organization, made better decisions, improved internal communications, looked at future job opportunities in a very different way, thought with a new perspective (because the coach was from a different background), built support for much better networking, cemented key relationships, and progressed more quickly than had been anticipated.

Individuals also reported on unexpected outcomes about personal development including the following examples: a stronger feeling of security and calm in dealing with difficult issues; a very pleasurable experience with lots of fun alongside the challenge; very focused conversations about themselves and their style of impacting on others; a much stronger level of self-assurance; a move from feeling miserable to being quite happy, and a much better sleeping pattern.

Many of the immediate benefits of coaching relate to influencing skills and personal impact on others. For example, Helen is a Finance Director in a multinational fast-moving consumer products business. The coach helped her to understand the full breadth of her role at this senior level. As a result of the coaching, she built an excellent network and acquired sponsors in strategic positions so she was able to deliver on her department's goals. She led cost-cutting and other unpopular programmes without damaging her relationships within the organization. Through the opportunity to stand back in the coaching, she grew in poise and authority and increased her influencing skills dramatically.

A further example was John, a new recruit to a senior team in a large international company who showed brash behaviour and 'got up people's noses', despite a strong performance and a clearly articulated visionary leadership. His behaviour was such that he was in danger of losing his job. The reality of the situation gradually began to sink in. The coach helped him to understand his impact on others and modify his behaviour so that he developed much stronger relationships of mutual respect with his team, his peers and the board. He was then, and only then, able to deliver on strategic goals, which he did so well that his job became secure and promotion to the main board became a serious possibility.

The overall effect of coaching can be to help an individual go from good to great. What coaching can do is to enable someone to stand back, helping them keep up with the strategic agenda and have the time to reflect. It is the dynamic engagement between coach and client that enables a lift-off to take place, so that an individual engages with the full range of opportunities in their role.

What is the experience like of being coached?

There are some basic requirements necessary to ensure success in a coaching relationship:

- **clarity** at the start about the expectations of the client organization and the client;
- **openness** in the client in identifying what areas they want to work on;
- **confidentiality** between the coach and the client about the content of the coaching discussions;
- **trust** and **respect** between coach and client;
- accurate **feedback** to the client from the organization about their own progress; and
- **hard work**: the client has to be willing to do the hard work of understanding themselves and others and be willing to risk experimenting with new approaches.

The above are fixed points in helping to ensure the coaching works successfully. They enable the coach to hold up a mirror with no distortions in the image. They are, however, just the basics. It is the quality of engagement over and above these minimum requirements that makes the difference between a good experience and a transformational experience.

The CEO of an asset management organization expressed the quality of engagement in relation to people in CEO posts in the following way:

> *'If his personal values and aspirations can be considered, weighed and, to a significant extent, dovetailed with his job, real enthusiasm will replace a sense of duty for the CEO as I have found, and the "feel good" factor will enhance his motivation enormously.'*

The following are examples of the experience of being coached, illustrating key themes.

Standing back to reflect

In the privacy of one-to-one conversations there is the opportunity to **stand back and reflect**. Alastair Redfern has worked with a coach since his appointment as Bishop of Derby was announced in mid 2005. The coaching conversations were initially about preparing for the new role and then have been working through key issues since Alastair became a Diocesan Bishop. His comments on the coaching are:

> 'The coaching helps me step back away from the job. Working with an external coach provides the additional distance which means that I can reflect more dispassionately about what I am doing than in conversations with anybody else. The coach brings their experience in management and leadership in very different organizations. In our conversations, we break down some of the issues and then put them back together again in a way that helps me decide on next steps. The coach gives me the type of questions but it is very much up to me to reach the conclusions. He never tells me what to do but enables me to think issues through.

> 'In the coaching conversations, the coach listens a lot, he helps me interpret some of the issues and enables me to articulate some of the strategic next steps. He brings a very different frame of reference. The conversations are always enjoyable, engaging and stretching. They help me look at things in new ways. I go out energized by the process and I look forward to the coaching conversations. I am always forced to think hard and come out of the conversations clearer in my own mind about my next steps.'

For Alastair, the coaching conversations involve hard thinking and a discipline of crystallizing with practical next steps. It is the opportunity to stand back and reflect with somebody from a very different world that is so powerful.

Understanding perceptions

George is a senior executive in a multinational energy organization. He is on the leadership team for one of the organization's business divisions and also on the functional leadership team for his professional discipline in the company. Those who have perspectives on his performance and capability come from many different nationalities. An all-round review took place and his coach interviewed ten people (bosses, subordinates, peers and a supplier).

The feedback of these perceptions about his strengths, motivations, performance and potential led to the following reaction from George:

> 'Receiving the feedback confirmed a lot of things for me. It also opened my eyes to one or two key items that I could then work on through coaching. I discovered that I was so preoccupied with getting things done because of the massive workload I have that I failed to see the broader impact I was (or rather wasn't!) having. I have now got a much better understanding of the important priorities I should be spending my time on, and try to delegate much more of my routine work.'

Facing up to key issues

Jenny has done a number of different jobs in a central government department. She had become gradually more frustrated with her role and had welcomed the opportunity to work in local government for a period. She relished this opportunity and was glad to be closer to the action in this new role. Coaching was helping her to face up to key issues. She described the contribution the coaching made during this period:

> 'The coaching was so helpful in enabling me to do this transition. The key thing was the nature of the questions. The coach asked difficult questions in a nice way. I never felt interrogated, but I was always being challenged. As a result of the coach's questions I would start resolving the issue. He pressed me to think through things that I didn't want to think about. Sometimes I just didn't want to face up to key issues, but he always seemed to identify what really mattered. The right questions were crucial. He would reflect back to me what I had been saying. He would comment 'you said' that I was terrible at doing certain things when there was clear evidence that I could do them. He made me realize how much I was putting myself down. He showed a mirror up to me. The outcome is I now do things differently. He helped me make the link between what I know and what I do. The coaching has been so powerful in enabling me to make a practical difference in the way I do things and the outcomes I am able to deliver. I was having difficulty with some staffing issues and, through conversations with the coach, I was able to address these issues in a completely different way.'

Jenny described the two most important features of successful coaching as:

- clarity about the nature of the coaching relationship at the start; and
- agreement that the relationship would be challenging both ways round: i.e. the coach should be able to challenge the coachee, but the coachee should also be able to challenge the coach in terms of how they were taking forward the coaching relationship.

Increasing personal impact

The experience of being coached for Garry, a director of a national organization, was principally about personal impact, key relationships and the opportunities that moving into a new role provided. Garry's comments on the coaching were:

> 'It made such a positive difference to me. I wondered if I would get something out of it. I came out of each conversation having developed some new ideas. There was always the wonderful surprise of something new and exciting that would come out of the discussion. At the end of each conversation I was always more self-aware and always positive. The coaching programme made a huge difference.'

Garry came to each coaching session with a sense of anticipation. There were always some particular things to discuss, but the experience of coaching meant a journey of discovery whereby new approaches and ideas grew out of the conversation, meaning that he was energized at the end with a commitment to action in specific areas.

Mike Whitaker, managing director in a major global investment bank, now responsible for the technology and e-commerce initiative for a key business found coaching impactful:

> 'Working with my coach gave me the awareness, skills and confidence to state what I wanted, set aggressive targets and have real impact in both my professional and personal life.'

Linking the facts of a situation and your emotional reactions to it

For Paul, Executive Director of a UK Strategic Health Authority, coaching has been no soft option. It has been important for him as he has moved from central government into a very different world. His comments on the coaching are:

'Coaching is often hard work. It puts you on your mettle. It adds value tactically at critical moments in your job and specifically when you feel becalmed. Coaching can help you take advantage of windows of opportunity when strategic decisions can be taken. Coaching can help in moments of building bridges between transactional and transformational. How can we bring together the facts of a situation and the emotional reactions to that situation? The most effective leaders have an appropriate degree of self-doubt; hence the value of reflecting with a third party when the benefits of self-doubt produce reflection and then sound action. A robust feedback loop at the next meeting holds me to account which helps ensure that I will do what I say I will do.'

Improving communications

Improving the ability to communicate effectively in a fast-changing world is vital. Coaching can play an important role in enabling an individual to be much more aware of the relative effectiveness of different forms of communication and to use targeted face-to-face communication to the best possible effect.

For Stan, the CFO in an industrial UK plc operating worldwide, his concern for the organization in its volatile market and his passion for results on top of a heavy workload meant that, instead of shaping his time to have regular face-to-face meetings, he fired off emails regularly to his CEO, the regional MDs and his finance team. They gained the impression that he was more the CEO than the CFO! This method of communication antagonized the CEO increasingly. Stan commented:

'Working through my thinking patterns and beliefs with my coach has helped me think through and reflect on both my and the CEO's motivations. Now I have a clear framework of how to respond. I have curbed my 'emailitis'. I am in the CFO role and know what's required. I have found the coaching process massively useful!'

Coaching helped Stan use a much wider range of communication approaches effectively.

Learning about yourself

There can be a 'light-going-on moment' in a coaching discussion, when an individual sees in their own mind what is holding them back. It might be a simple acknowledgement that they should stop banging their head against a brick wall; it might be fully internalizing a strength they had not appreciated before; it might be moving on and stopping being a victim.

When Peter talked with a group of clergymen who felt beleaguered with the prospect of change, the 'light-going-on moment' was when they accepted that they could either continue to enjoy their resentment or move on. They accepted that they needed to stop wallowing in feeling hard-done-by. Any feeling of resentment was their problem and not the Bishop's.

A 'light-going-on moment' for Julie was when she accepted that her staff cared as much as she did. Julie felt she had to rush around doing everything; eventually she accepted that this was unrealistic. The defining moment came from both recognizing the practicalities and fully accepting the learning about herself: that being driven to do everything herself was detrimental to herself, her work and her staff.

What happens in a coaching discussion?

A coaching discussion is a journey of discovery, with clarity of objectives at the start and first steps on a route map. The focus needs to be clear on important outcomes. Sometimes there will be roadblocks and the route has got to change, or the traffic will be such that there will be time to reflect, or the pace will have to go faster.

Good coaching conversations have clarity but lots of flexibility too. Beverley is a lawyer and has grown hugely in confidence as a result of the coaching she received. Beverley talks of the coaching in these words:

> *'The coach seems to know what is concerning me. Because of his experience and the way he reads me, he has a clear insight into what I am thinking. He then draws out these issues and helps me to address them. The coaching makes me face up to issues I want to camouflage. The coach has been brilliant in helping me look at issues from other people's perspectives. He had helped me understand why they behaved like they did. He has got me to realize what is going on in their minds. It has enabled me to go into a difficult conversation in a much more confident way, and helped me to get the right responses. I don't always see the point until after the coaching sessions, but then the value of the coaching is so obvious. The coach would often use pictures, like getting me to think about the foundation I am building. He would help me build up my confidence before going into key meetings. The coach got me to think about climbing a mountain and saying why I was on the climb. The simple question of where did other people higher up the mountain start to climb is a very powerful metaphor, but everyone started at*

the bottom. Coaching has made me more confident and allowed me to grow. The coach has helped me to bring out my own talents. The process enabled me to identify where I lacked confidence. It has helped break the cycle and ensure that I have a much better toolkit for dealing with difficult situations. The coaching is standing me in good stead for the next stages of my career. The lessons from coaching keep ringing in my head. I am much more able to deal with new situations in a confident, positive way as a result of the coaching.'

What happens in a coaching conversation is a contributor to wider changes. When an individual views a situation positively, they will take additional opportunities to master that situation and build support in a variety of ways. The coaching conversation might be the turning point, but it can only be one contributory factor. Ceri Smith is a senior administrator. His perspective is this:

'It is difficult to isolate the effects of coaching. You cannot identify a precise causal link. But the effect of the coaching has contributed significantly to my getting the world into perspective. It means I am much more comfortable about success and failure. I can balance in a much more rational way short-term failure against long-term success. I recognize now that some failure is not critical: it is about learning effectively through it. The coaching has allowed me to look at and dissect my management toolkit and to decide how to use it in a much more focused way. I am now more self-aware in how to manage because I can identify key issues more effectively. The discussions have allowed me to self-reflect in a way I have never done before. The coach helps me achieve a critical distance and think in new ways to identify things I might reflect on. It has enabled me to move on. I am much more comfortable in myself as a leader and have made significant progress, which has been reflected in both my performance assessment and in my own job satisfaction.'

Jagdev Singh Virdee (Dev), a senior official in a government department, talks of the most powerful coaching meeting being one that was three-way involving him, his boss and the coach. This discussion came at a critical moment and enabled there to be a full conversation about matters that needed to be resolved. This was an opportunity to define a shared agenda and to ensure a common awareness of how different issues were perceived. As a result there was a greater clarity about priorities and deadlines. Dev moved on significantly in his level of confidence over this period. His comments are:

'The coaching discussions provided time to think and talk things through with someone who was both supportive and challenging and work issues through to conclusion. It was invaluable to have somebody there who was on your side, whose only motive was to help you. It was invaluable to be able to explore a whole range of aspects of life: the result was a significant improvement in my personal wellbeing and effectiveness, which benefited both my impact at work and progress in other parts of my life.'

Coaching as dynamic conversation

At the heart of a good coaching discussion is a dynamic conversation. The best of conversations are dynamic, purposeful and warm: they engage, discern and stretch. Effective engagement in conversation is about:

- building trust and engendering openness;
- providing stillness amidst conversation to give people an opportunity to reflect;
- using humour to see the funny side of situations; and
- making conversation a shared journey of discovery.

Discernment is about:

- clarity of purpose in entering a conversation;
- questions that open up issues rather than close them down;
- curiosity; aiming to understand why a particular issue is important to somebody;
- experimentation so that we are not always predictable creatures of habit;
- taking risks in terms of sharing; and
- brevity in drawing out clear points and conclusions.

Stretching is about conversations that:

- are dynamic: you cannot predict the end of a conversation at the start;
- include a healthy level of debate while working through difficult issues;
- transcend boundaries and provide challenge so that conversations are not inward looking or comfortable;
- bring freshness and express things in different ways; and
- include a compelling modesty with a strong focus on listening.

At the heart of successful coaching are conversations between two people on a shared journey, which leads through exploration to discovery, conclusions and action. *

The importance of clarity of objectives

It is crucial for both the organization and the individual that there is a shared agenda about objectives. The following are examples of objectives for two senior members of a government department and two executives in the private sector. For Carol, the areas agreed at the start of the coaching were:

- developing her business plan and personal priorities;
- developing and making the most of key relationships;
- ensuring personal impact on policy development and delivery; and
- maximizing the learning in the job.

For Mohammed the areas agreed for focus were:

- leading through influence rather than management;
- building networks and partnerships within the regional office;
- developing skills to contribute effectively at a national level; and
- developing a greater assertiveness in his contribution when it was outside his natural comfort zone.

For Mike, the goals and objectives of the assignment were:

- learning how to become more hands off in leadership of larger numbers and to 'raise the game' by delegating even more;
- influencing and directing his management team effectively and handling succession issues in a timely fashion; and
- developing strategies for where he wants to take his business and how to engage his management team in their implementation.

For John, the agenda had a distinctly personal business focus:

- to transition the UK business effectively from a functional to a regional structure and show confidence and authority in doing so;

* Explained further in Peter Shaw's book *Conversation Matters: how to engage effectively with one another* (Continuum, 2005)

- to re-establish trust with the CEO; and
- to learn to be more proactive than reactive to an in-tray.

For all these people it was a regular return to these objectives that provided a discipline for the coaching, while at the same time they looked at issues that were particularly current to them at the time when the coaching discussion took place.

Clarity of feedback

The ideal is for the line manager to give clear feedback orally, but a coach can act as an intermediary in setting that stage. Many organizations now have written feedback tools that can be useful in giving a relative sense of what is going well or less well.

A potent tool is the use of oral feedback, whereby a skilled coach will ask an individual's boss, peers, key interlocutors and key staff for their perspectives. Sometimes this is best done in a very open-ended way through the use of a set of prompts such as, 'What might X do more of?' and, 'What might X do less of?'. An alternative can be something which is more focused to an individual's particular circumstances, such as questions like, 'What adjectives would you use to describe Y?' or, 'How well does she influence (upwards, key stakeholders, clients)?'. Depending on the situation there could be even more specific questions like, 'How does he make decisions?' or, 'What is his particular contribution in group meetings?'

To be done well, oral feedback must be gathered by a coach who can immediately gain the respect of those whom he is meeting. A coach has got to know when to press the interviewee about what they mean by particular comments in order to extract maximum benefit from the conversation. There needs to be a good immediate level of engagement between the coach and the individuals the coach is interviewing, so that each individual both wants to contribute and is honest in doing so.

Good questions in oral 360° feedback can get to the root of behaviours so that the coaching can work on the aspects that are going to make the biggest difference. The good coach will not take every answer at face value: they will want to go behind the initial answer. This reinforces the value of skilled questioning through oral 360° feedback, enabling much deeper issues to be identified and put into context than is possible through standardized written 360° feedback approaches.

Oral 360° feedback repeated after a year can give a very powerful measure of how somebody has developed over the intervening period. It is surprising how reluctant people can be to exposing themselves to 360° oral feedback, but our experience is that it is the most powerful device for getting to the bottom of important issues that need to be resolved.

The effective matching of coach and client

An important step is getting the right match between coach and coachee. The chemistry has got to be right for the relationship to work well. There needs to be a pretty instant rapport, whereby the individual feels both at home with the coach and open to the reality that a good coaching conversation will be stretching. Key questions are whether the individual will respond better to someone who has a similar or very different background, brings extensive leadership experience or comes from a more psychologically based approach, is of a similar or different age, and is of the same gender or the opposite gender.

The effective matching of coach and client may mean there is one lead coach with other coaches being brought in for specific sessions to draw upon their particular expertise. Coaching relationships can run out of steam after a period, so the effective translation at the right time from one coach to another can be important if momentum is not to be lost.

The impact of coaching across an individual's life

Coaching funded by an organization is primarily about meeting the needs of the employing organization. Effective coaching will have an impact on an individual's wellbeing and influence across the whole of their life. If an individual is able to prioritize their time and energy more effectively, this will benefit both the employing organization, the individual's colleagues and their family. Effective coaching transcends boundaries between different spheres of an individual's life in a way that is constructive and never indulgent. Successful approaches in coaching discussions will lock together professional and personal dimensions. Peter often uses the framework of the 4 'V's of 'Vision, Values, Value-added and Vitality'*.

His belief is that, for an individual to move forward, there needs to be a linking together of these four areas. Why?

- **Vision**. This enables us to be very clear about who we want to be. What is the essential Wendy-ness, Mark-ness or Mohammed-ness? What is the

---

* Explained further in Peter Shaw's book *The Four Vs of Leadership: Vision, Values, Value-added and Vitality* (Capstone, 2006)

coherence of our vision of ourselves that brings together our work, community and home personalities into one coherent person?

- **Values**. What are the values that drive us? Do we understand where they came from and how they are changing? How can we harness our values to help our own fulfilment and the wellbeing of those around us? How do we ensure our values are our biggest asset and not our worst liability?
- **Value-added**. What are our strengths? How can we develop them and use them to the best effect? What are we less good at? How can we develop skills in those areas? How can we become more confident in adding value in a wider range of different situations? How can we add value in all our interactions with different people so that they are enlightened and encouraged?
- **Vitality**. What is at the heart of what gives us energy? Can we grow that source of energy? Can we take it into different areas of our lives? What is the interlink between what gives us energy at home and in our parallel worlds of family, community, faith, arts or sport? How can those sources of energy flow back into our work situations? What part does stillness play in nurturing our sources of energy?

The 4 'V's can help an individual:

- become more focused in their personal vision and potentially equip them for a wider range of different jobs;
- become more explicit in defining their values and in reassessing their life priorities against those values;
- become clearer about their value-added contributions and enable them to delegate more effectively; and
- reassess how they use their energy, enabling them to spend more time on activities that are most important to them, which will raise their vitality.

The starting points for this approach are:

- does your personal vision need a change (maybe it is too vague or too rigid)?
- do your values influence you in the ways you want?
- is your value-added in different spheres needing to change?
- is your vitality a bit squashed or randomly directive?

Working through the 4 'V's has been applied successfully with people in a range of different organizations and has lead to a whole range of different next steps such as:
- taking forward specific aspects of personal vision;

- focusing on two or three key values and looking at how they are applied across each aspect of life;
- being more precise about defining the value-added an individual wants to bring and what impact could be made in a range of different contexts; and
- being more self-aware about the reasons for different levels of vitality and how specific sources of vitality can be grown.

If an individual is able effectively to interrelate their values and aspirations across different spheres of their life, they are likely to be both successful in a work context and more fulfilled in their personal life. This is, however, in the context that the prime purpose of coaching must be for the benefit of the employing organization.

Conclusion

What a coachee gets out of coaching is dependent on the commitment of the individual and the employing organization, the quality of the input of the coach, and the dynamic nature of the engagement. There needs to be a dynamic creative engagement that is fresh, fun and focused. Clarity of objectives and outcomes play an important part. Good-quality feedback to the individual, handled sensitively, is vital. A robustness of relationship depends on the effective matching of coach and coachee, which may well mean complementary skills and experience rather than a matching of like for like.

The quality of the coaching can only be as good as the nature of the engagement between the participants, with the full support of the employing organization. This support needs to be a strength of commitment to the benefits of coaching whilst ensuring the confidentiality of the coaching relationship. This involves the employing organization having a strong trust in the quality of the coaches and the coaching organizations that it employs.

Chapter 6:

Different Formats for Coaching

This chapter explores different formats of coaching, covering:

- one-to-one coaching with an external coach;
- one-to-one coaching with an internal coach;
- team coaching;
- learning sets;
- one-to-one coaching on specific skills;
- group coaching on specific skills;
- dual coach coaching;
- co-coaching;
- telephone coaching; and
- developing a coaching culture.

It illustrates the wealth of different formats for coaching, with the key starting point being clarity about the overall business needs and the needs of different people or groups within the organization. A common theme that runs through all these formats of coaching is effective engagement between coach and client that is responsive to their evolving needs.

There are is wide range of different types of coaching relationships which are summarized in Fig. 6.1. These are complementary and will be relevant in different ways at different times. Here are some key questions.

- How different are people's individual circumstances?
- Will group learning enhance or inhibit?
- Which of these different approaches fit the needs of the organization best?

Fig. 6.1 Different types of coaching relationships

One-to-one coaching with an external coach

This book is principally about this type of coaching. The benefits of the one-to-one relationship are the confidentiality, the personal quality of the relationship, and the nature of the support and challenge which can be specifically geared to an individual's circumstances. An individual is much more likely to open up about their particular issues if it is in the safe environment of a one-to-one relationship. But the success of this coaching depends so much on the qualities of the coach and their ability to take somebody out of their comfort zone and strengthen their resolve to take forward difficult issues.

The value of an external coach is that they bring a wealth of experience from different worlds. Where a coach has had extensive experience at senior levels themselves, they can bring a perspective which can be invaluable. The coach who has led major change management themselves and has experienced the joys and frustrations at first hand is likely to be in a much better position to be able to empathize with an individual going through a similar situation. The limited knowledge that an external coach will have of a particular organization is both a strength and a potential weakness. The external coach who is used to working in a range of different organizations will bring an objective perspective that can help the client see issues through new eyes. The good coach will pick up the key features of an organization quickly and will not be inhibited by their lack of specific knowledge. Many individuals talk of the benefit of working with a coach who is not immersed in a particular environment: they welcome that degree of distance combined with a wide range of understanding.

One-to-one coaching with an internal coach

A number of larger organizations have set up an internal coaching capacity. The strengths of these arrangements are that internal coaches know the business well, can focus the coaching on specific business needs, have a strong appreciation of the expectations of senior management, are flexible in their availability and may be cheaper than an external coach. They may see the client in action or have feedback from a range of people on a regular basis about how the individual is progressing. The disadvantages are that internal coaches will have less width of experience, are unlikely to have the seniority of experience of some external coaches, and may not have the same objectivity or the same freedom of perspective as an external coach.

Two significant factors determine the success of internal coaches, however qualified they may be.

1 *Culture.* The culture of the organization becomes transparent in the coaching relationship involving two employees. How open and trusting is the environment? How hierarchical? To what extent is assessment important as well as development of the individual client? What written documentation will there be and how will it be used? These are just some of the questions that need to be addressed before coaching can take place effectively.
2 *Level requiring coaching.* A board member or senior divisional director in a large enterprise will often have great difficulty in sharing both the organization's commercial and strategic agenda and their own personal fears/concerns/intentions with someone who is not another board member or a trusted independent adviser. Confidentiality at this level of the organization is a key requirement in any discussion.

Internal coaching often works most powerfully with more junior staff and when there are specific business needs that need addressing. If there is a development need common to a significant number of staff, internal coaching based on a particular formula can have a marked impact.

An organization does not necessarily have to choose between one-to-one coaching with an external coach and one-to-one coaching with internal coaches. Within the same organization, external coaching might be the most effective tool for senior staff and those whose key relationships are external, while internal coaching might work best for junior staff addressing specific development needs.

Team coaching

Team coaching can work equally well for the board of a multinational organization or a team leading a particular project. Effective team coaching needs the same type of physical context as individual coaching, i.e. a quiet, confidential environment with adequate time for people to think, reflect and be challenged. Effective team coaching often has the aims of clarifying objectives, defining priority areas, considering how well the senior team operates and building commitment about next steps.

Team coaching needs to start from a clear understanding of current reality, which might be based on interviews with a cross section of staff, the perceptions of key partners or customers or the views of individual members of the team. Having a clear understanding of the strengths and areas for development within the team is key.

An important next step is a clear understanding of the vision or outcomes sought, with a testing of the reality and boldness of that vision. The coach working with the team needs then to be able to draw out how strongly the agenda is shared, what the most important next steps are, what is going to be the value-added of each member of the team, how the wider organization is going to be brought into the next steps on taking forward the vision, what the sources of energy are for each member of the team and how effectively the team is going to both support and challenge each other.

With team coaching, a key strand is often going to be about how the individuals react together and how they interact with others, leaders in the organization and stakeholders. The good team coach is not only addressing the functional nature but also the emotional dynamics of the relationships. At the end of a good team coaching session there will be new energy and the embracing of each other's hopes and aspirations.

When team coaching is working well, the coach is acting more as a facilitator than a coach, with individual members of the team playing an important role in stretching each other in an environment where they are each committed to each other's success. The good team coach will have all the skills of a one-to-one coach with the additional strands of reading group dynamics well, drawing in members of the team, understanding how best to encourage and stretch individual members and enabling both a reflective and lively level of discussion between members.

Patrick Lencioni in his book *The Five Dysfunctions of a Team* (Jossey-Bass) talks of the five themes of:

- absence of trust;
- fear of conflict;
- lack of commitment;
- avoidance of accountability; and
- inattention to results.

A skilled coach can help a team explore these areas and help a team reach a stage where the members more readily trust each other, engage in unfiltered debate about issues, commit wholeheartedly to shared decisions and agendas and focus on the achievement of collective results. The good team coach has to be able to process several individual's agendas at once to enable the whole team to move on.

Learning sets

Learning sets can be a particularly valuable way of learning from peers. The best learning sets bring together people from different environments who have some strong, shared perspectives or interests. Ellie was part of a learning set for a couple of years. She commented:

> 'We are part of a learning set that is magical, which is much more than the sum of its parts. How do we know that it has been successful? Because we all want to be there. We go away with new ideas and fresh energy. We can share work dynamism and personal concerns in a safe environment. We go away uplifted, feeling much more positive. We want to share with each other. At the same time we feel challenged by the other participants. That challenge is not just in one meeting: in a subsequent meeting we will be held to account for the actions we committed ourselves to take in the preceding conversation.'

Ellie is clear about what makes a learning set work effectively. Her views are:

> 'You need to **prepare**: some thought, however short, needs to go into what needs to be discussed. You have to **be present**: this is more about attitude and goes to the heart of what learning sets are all about, which is offering support and encouragement as well as being a critical friend. You have to **participate**: you need to contribute even though the issue or dilemma may not be the one you have experienced. A key lesson for me is that we can all add value in our own way.'

Beverley and Jenny were part of a learning set for high-potential younger staff, with a coach as a facilitator, over a couple of years. They both regarded the group as a great success. Beverley described how she had initially been sceptical and then the group had taken off. Beverley described the characteristics of the group as 'its openness and honesty, with individuals gradually sharing more of the trust that had been built up'.

At the end of a couple of years' working together, each of the members gave feedback about their colleagues in terms of what they most appreciated about them and what they thought were their continuing areas of development. This feedback was done thoughtfully in a way that built up each individual's confidence. The feedback was given in a warm and encouraging way, while identifying key issues that individuals needed to continue to work on. The feedback was all the more powerful and valuable because it was given in a spirit of caring for each other. Beverley said, 'It was as if we had a stake in each other's future and success.'

Jenny was clear that the feedback could not have worked right at the start of the learning set. Ownership of the process was so important. Jenny described how the group got to a stage when they realized that it was *their* group, they owned how it was organized and they felt open enough to share their individual experiences of success and failure. For Jenny there was a particular joy in seeing people grow and change and satisfaction in having helped in that process.

A key question is what is the lasting effect of participating in this sort of learning set. For Jenny, the experience means that she would be more positive about opening up in new groups and be ready to learn from other people at an earlier stage. For Beverley, it was crucial to keep embedding the learning so that the confidence she gained in one group was transferred to her ability to work effectively in another group.

Learning sets need champions to be effective. Someone has to put in the energy to ensure the arrangements work well. There needs to be a shared commitment among members to give a high priority to being part of the set. Ideally a learning set has a facilitator who plays a low-key role in steering a conversation so that members are supportive and coaching each other. An important gift in a facilitator is knowing when to let a conversation run and when to move it on. The crucial engagement is how the coach moves in and out of the conversation, to steer it and then read the signals about when it is right to move on.

One-to-one coaching on specific skills

A lot of executive coaching is about overall performance and behavioural issues. Sometimes the need is for specific-skills coaching in such areas as giving a major presentation, working with a specific group of customers, developing more of an impact in specific types of meetings or projecting their voice more clearly. This may involve the targeted use of, say, three sessions.

In such areas, the use of specialist trainers can be effective, with the advantage of a clarity of focus on a particular skill need. What is so important is that specialist trainers use a coaching style that enables the individual to develop their skills in an expressive and enjoyable way. Work done by organizations employing actors to demonstrate dramatic techniques has had a powerful influence on high-potential individuals wanting to make a step-change in their personal impact. An individual may well benefit from one-to-one work or group work on a specific issue with a trainer, complemented by work with a coach on how these skills are implemented and discussion about the learning that has taken place as new approaches have been applied.

Group coaching on specific skills

Where an organization identifies a strong need to improve performance in particular generic skills, bringing individuals together in workshops can be an effective way forward. These workshops need to have clear objectives and must be structured to allow participants to test out their ideas, learn from the experiences of colleagues, and go away with some clear ideas to try out in their day job. As illustrations, here are the frameworks for three group-coaching workshops which addressed specific needs within a national organization:

A: Influencing, persuading and building key relationships

Themes

- What is your preferred influencing style: how can you use and stretch your preferred style?
- How can you become more flexible in your styles of influence and approach
- What influencing approaches of leaders do you admire, and how can you embrace some of that learning?
- What persuasion techniques work best in different practical situations?
- What key relationships are most important to you and how do you want to build those relationships?
- How can you see things from the other person's perspective?

Outcomes

- Better listening skills;
- Increased ability to think inside another person's shoes;
- Clearer and wider range of influencing skills;
- The ability to use focused conversation as a powerful took in a wide range of circumstances;
- Greater confidence in developing key relationships both inside and outside the organization;
- Developing productive relationships for the longer term; and
- Better awareness of individual situations.

B: Leading change and raising the performance of your team

Themes

- Recognising the key ingredients of leading successful change;
- The relevance of the values set out by the Chief Executive and the board;
- Taking the initiative in enabling transitions to work effectively;
- Raising the performance of your team;
- Using delegation more effectively;
- Understanding what holds people back from making change; and
- The importance of wellbeing in self and others.

Outcomes

- Clarity about the next steps in leading change;
- A toolkit to develop your leadership skills;
- The ability to give and receive feedback effectively;
- The ability to handle challenging conversations well;
- A greater emotional awareness of the perspectives of members of your team; and
- Greater confidence in holding others and yourself accountable.

C: Making difficult decisions[*]

Themes

- Effective ways of handling difficult decisions (covering policy, operations, staffing, time priorities and personal impact);
- Learning from how others make difficult decisions;
- Using case studies from an individual's own experience to develop decision-making skills and capabilities; and
- Developing the confidence to make difficult decisions.

Outcomes

- Greater confidence in making and living with difficult decisions;
- The ability to be tougher when necessary;
- The use of a framework enabling the participant to plan their way through difficult decisions; and
- Developing the capacity in each individual to be more confident in aspects of decision making that do not come easily to them.

In designing group coaching, it is crucial that the themes are directly relevant to the organization. Ideally, the participants shape the themes either before or at the start of the workshops. The atmosphere in the workshops needs to be one of mutual sharing and support: the greater the freedom to share personal experience, the greater the prospect of personal learning that is fresh and embedded.

---

[*] This will be developed further in Peter Shaw's book *Making Difficult Decisions* (Capstone, to be published in 2008)

The skills needed in group coaching include understanding issues quickly and being able to draw people out through building trust, but also challenging them to move on in their thinking and be robust about next steps.

Coaching linked to personal development plans

There can be a discontinuity between an organization's performance-management arrangements and coaching. Aligning the two is important if coaching is going to lead to significant behavioural change.

As an example, a Health Authority wanted to ensure that the preparation of Personal Development Plans was done in a focused and practical way. They adopted the approach of asking all 15 members of the Senior Team to have one-to-one coaching sessions with an external coach to help each of them develop their Personal Development Plan. After the coaches had been briefed about the particular business needs of the organization, the first coaching discussion was about what might go in the Personal Development Plan. The second discussion was working through a draft of the individual's Personal Development Plan, helping to give it focus. In these discussions, the coach acted as a sounding board and a source of challenge.

Each individual then discussed their Personal Development Plan with the Chief Executive. All of the participants welcomed the focus on preparing rigorous Personal Development Plans and welcomed the involvement of an external coach. The organization regarded this as a cost-effective approach to bringing the benefits of coaching to all its senior staff in a way that was going to lead to the best impact on the performance of the organization.

Dual-coach coaching

In business coaching, we often find that clients have specific items on their agenda which need to be pursued on a one-to-one basis. Some aspects of that agenda are more relevant to another coach and can be handled more specifically by another coach. The 'lead coach' or principal will seek out a colleague to work on such aspects. Here are two examples of this.

- The client will be seeking specific feedback in a particular area, e.g. creativity or conflict-resolution handling and the principal coach does not have the relevant knowledge of psychometrics which could be used. The coach can then engage a colleague with relevant experience and skills who might use a relevant psychometric instrument and give relevant feedback.

- The client may have a specific need in an area of business which needs to be explored in depth (e.g. mergers and acquisitions) where a coach with specific experience might be brought in for a few specific sessions.

Co-coaching

When two individuals have been through a coaching programme and are in similar spheres, co-coaching can play a part in taking forward next steps. For example, two Chairs of Health Authorities who had been through a coaching programme agreed that they would meet periodically, with the topics for discussion being issues like working with the Chief Executive, getting the best out of board members, ensuring a constructive relationship with key partners and focusing on the value-added one brought as the Chair. They agreed that ways of approaching the discussions could cover the following questions.

- What am I finding most frustrating?
- What are the most difficult decisions I'm facing?
- What is most painful about the actions I need to take?
- What are the next steps that might be most beneficial?

They agreed to share topics in advance that they would discuss. They decided to have discussions that would be structured in their format, followed up by an informal meal together. This helped them keep up the discipline of thinking hard about their priorities and the use of the energy that had come out of the one-to-one coaching.

Telephone coaching

The power of coaching is what goes on in the conversation between two individuals. Normally that is best done face-to-face where there can be eye-to-eye contact. The best coaching relationships involve regular face-to-face contact supplemented by telephone conversations at key moments, where there is a focused issue that needs to be talked about. This can be such a powerful combination: a phone call at the start of a busy day can help the individual be much more focused about their priorities for a major meeting. Telephone coaching can be a very valuable supplement.

Both of us coach people via telephone conversations having had some initial face-to-face discussions. Because there is strong personal contact already, telephone coaching works perfectly well. Telephone coaching can be a very disciplined way of working through specific issues. Humour and silence can work just as well on the phone, provided the participants feel relaxed and enjoy using this approach. It is well worth trying telephone discussion as a supplement to face-to-face discussion as a way of working through more immediate issues.

We have both done telephone coaching where we have not met the individual. It can still be effective when both participants feel they can engage well without having met and are able to find a level of humour that works, but there is a dimension potentially missing, which is picking up the non-verbal signals from the client.

Robin has been coaching a client in Hong Kong over the telephone who has engaged fully in the agenda he has wanted to pursue, namely how to establish himself as newly appointed chief executive and how to identify the priorities for the first six months in office. Relevant background material included feedback and his observations from a leadership programme he attended at an international business school. The focus of the coaching was on some key personal development items. The coach's discussions with other directors, which he has recorded in writing and 're-played' over the phone, have added to this. The business agenda is being played out in the press and this has brought the coaching into bas-relief!

Both of us coach people living in other continents. A 90-minute coaching discussion can be just as effective by telephone once a personal relationship is established. Peter and Andrew McDonald have been working together for over a year whilst Andrew has been based in California and Peter has been working in London. Andrew's comments on coaching at a distance are:

> 'Before leaving for California I wasn't sure how telephone coaching would work. Would it seem awkward? Would a 90-minute call seem a bit long and the format a bit artificial? It soon became clear that it was going to be fine. Peter and I had struck up a strong relationship before I headed off so we had something to draw on: we knew and trusted one another. The telephone conversations flowed naturally and provided me with just the stimulus I needed to shape my development work during my sabbatical. I am not sure it would have worked any better if we had been in the same room. If anything, I found myself listening even harder to what Peter said because I wasn't able to pick up any visual cues from him. I would strongly recommend telephone coaching – but only if you first meet the coach and have a chance to get to know him or her.'

Developing a coaching culture

Every organization in its own way will seek to 'ratchet up' performance so that the business can increase, grow and continually get the best results possible. For many organizations, this 'process' is seen as creating an environment or culture in which people are stretched, challenged and developed. The creation of a 'coaching culture' in this way has both an external and an internal dynamic. Treating internal customers in the same way as external customers can be one of the benefits of developing a coaching culture.

When it comes to corporate governance, there are external and internal stakeholders in a business – in terms of customer service, the internal colleagues who are part of the production and supply chain are as much customers as those external customers who buy the goods and pay you the money. In the same way, the approach and attitude towards development of external stakeholders should characterize the approach and attitude to internal stakeholders.

A valuable part of any coaching relationship is developing coaching skills in the client so that they can use some of their learning in the way they work with their team. This is often particularly about developing skills in the use of questioning to enable the line manager to draw out next steps on particular issues from their direct reports, rather than being explicit about next steps. Widening the repertoire of a senior manager to include coaching skills does not remove the need for directive leadership in particular situations, but it can have an important influence in widening the effectiveness of an individual's leadership approaches. The good coach is asking in coaching sessions how the learning an individual has experienced about coaching can be embedded in the way they lead their staff.

Conclusion

There is a wealth of different formats for coaching, with a clear need to distinguish what approach is going to be most helpful in a particular situation. A strategy for coaching in an organization may well start with one-to-one coaching from experienced external coaches, supplemented by team- or group-level coaching addressing cross-cutting issues. The starting point must be clarity about the overall business needs, the particular needs of different people or groups of people in the organization, and the steps that can best address those needs.

Chapter 7:

Coaching Starts at the Top

This chapter looks specifically at the relevance of coaching for the senior leader in an organization, which might be the Chief Executive, Director General or Managing Partner. It looks at:
- stepping up to be the Chief Executive;
- examples of coaching of Chief Executives;
- the potential advantage of coaching for Chief Executives, covering new-to-post; stretching the thinking; becoming more strategic; having a sounding board; testing out specific strategies and clarity abut ultimate responsibility;
- enabling an individual to prepare to become a Chief Executive;
- meeting reservations from Chief Executives; and
- taking forward coaching for Chief Executives.

Our perspective is that good coaching for the Chief Executive can make a significant difference to an individual in a lonely and often precarious place.

The senior leader in an organization may be called the Chief Executive, Managing Director, Director General or Managing Partner. For simplicity, we use the term Chief Executive. The personal accountability for decision making is firmly on their shoulders. There is no hiding place.

Stepping up to be Chief Executive

The Chief Executive is in a very different situation to any other leader within an organization. They have to manage the long-term viability of an enterprise in an environment where performance is measured against short-term targets, which puts a unique pressure on the CEO. This pressure can be particularly acute in a plc where the board chair may be focused on the short term because of the interests of shareholders while the CEO is striving to address longer-term challenges.

As the focus of attention, the CEO has the dual responsibilities for the measurable delivery and the behavioural characteristics of the organization. The CEO is the role model to whom everyone in the business looks for both the business vision and the demonstration of living the values they espouse. It is a very lonely place being the role model whom people want to both admire and criticize. The CEO is expected to be the exemplar of both business focus and standards: they are always on show to staff, stakeholders and customers.

The transformation to CEO often means that the individual has to deal with a completely new set of questions. These are fundamental corporate-strategy questions about the institution itself. The questions in corporate life often end up as sophisticated finance and communications questions, which require new knowledge and very specific skills – but they are, no matter what institution, about the value and validity of the institution itself: how it justifies the investment in it by its paymasters, either public or private; and how it continues to do so in the light of their changing needs and competitive pressures for that money or resource. It means addressing the question, 'Why do I deserve more investment than others?'

These questions are often not really thought about until the individual gets close to, or even in, the job. They exacerbate the sense of loneliness because other colleagues mostly don't have to engage with them – so it is not just the number, but the nature of the stakeholders which is critical.

For the Chief Executive, there are a myriad of dimensions that effect their accountability, some of which are summarized in Fig. 7.1. The Chief Executive has to engage effectively with each of these dimensions.

Each strand of this diagram is important: all of them have to be working well. At the heart of success is credibility, fully understanding the changing context, leading and not following the debate and being a strong source of vision and energy.

Such are the expectations of a Chief Executive, and the gap between success and failure so short, that investment in good-quality coaching can result in significant dividends. Rather than being a luxury, good coaching support for a Chief Executive is an invaluable investment.

Examples of coaching of Chief Executives

Some examples where coaching has been particularly applicable follow.

Fig. 7.1 Factors involved in a Chief Executive's accountability

- The CEO in an IT company had seen the company go through an entre-preneurial growth phase. Now he had to build in proper process in the organization. He was into everything and kept seeking reassurance and approval from his direct reports, to the extent that this was getting in the way of effective business relationships. The coach talked to a number of the CRE's direct reports and made him face up to the fact that he was perceived as a bully. This led to his developing a very different approach, which took the company into a successful second phase.
- A new CEO who had formerly been the Finance Director was now push-ing major change across the organization. He had never had experience of building a team in this wide way. He was in his mid fifties, and in this role he needed to develop a range of skills different to those that had made him a successful Finance Director. His approach, developed over a number of years, was to be lean and mean with an aggressive streak. He now had to grow synergies between businesses, which meant building a team of geographically disparate business leaders who were willing to

share expertise across the group. The coaching enabled him to adapt his personal approach so he developed his skills in collaboration. He was still strong at challenging, but built up his capacity to be supportive as well. What helped him change his approach was seeing clearly the need to do so and developing a better understanding of what was likely to motivate the senior leadership group.

- Another CEO was long-established and people were getting a bit bored with him. He needed to develop a different leadership style to grab their attention and bring people on in a very different way: he needed to bring more creativity and energy. He and the coach role-played a variety of different approaches. They talked hard about where his energy came from and how he could raise the vitality levels in some of his senior team. The result was a conscious step-change in approach, which meant his senior leaders did 'sit up and think' and were more strongly influenced by his leadership.
- Another individual had just become the Managing Partner in a professional organization. In this professional world, she needed to lead by influence and not control. She needed to be much more conscious of the impact she had on others and how she could use the high esteem in which she was held to generate focused change in the organization. The coach interviewed a range of people who had worked with her to build a picture of the impact she had on them. The result was a clear picture that enabled the client to decide how she wanted to moderate her approach. Working through different strategies with her coach enabled her to take on a new approach, which proved to be successful.
- The new Chief Executive was a woman with young children, who was trying to balance different pressures on her time. She needed to be highly disciplined in the use of time and selective in how she was going to be involved in the business. There were no easy choices. The coaching helped her to identify the choices and work through the implications in a very objective and dispassionate way.
- The CEO was moving into a very different context. His career had seen him go into a series of different situations and sort them out: he had fixed things and then moved on. Now he had set up an operation and had to run it and was not going to be moving on. He had built the team he wanted but was disappointed they were not performing effectively. He had never had to motivate and inspire a team before. The individuals were so competitive that they did not talk to each other. He introduced a degree of matrix working to create a culture of mutual responsibility. The CEO's learning, developed through the coaching, was about how his behaviours affected the behaviours of his senior team. He learnt how patience sometimes needs to sit alongside focused energy.

Jon Little was the Chief Executive and now is Chairman of Mellon Global Investments. He described his experience of coaching as a Chief Executive in the following ways.

- *How has coaching helped you as a business leader?* It has helped me make better decisions. Just stopping and talking through the issue and situation is helpful. Some discussions you cannot have easily with those you are working with. I have been able to test-run ideas with an independent person. If you test ideas on your team, they are immediately thinking about how it affects them. If you test ideas on your boss, it can colour the next steps right from the start. Thinking through the consequences with an independent person is so very helpful. The shaping of my team partly came from coaching discussions.
- *Have there been different benefits at different points?* Some of the benefits come when I try to explain a situation and it doesn't seem to fit together. That gives me the opportunity to go back and start again. The intelligent questioning of the coach is very helpful. When the coaching began, we were dealing with current, immediate and tactical issues. Now that I know where I am going on these, we have moved much more into a forward-looking dimension. The coach will ask me how I am getting on with particular issues and press me on what I have done to help make things happen and what I need to do in the future to ensure the right changes occur. The coach is good at asking questions about implications of decisions and posing questions about whether there is a better way.
- *How would you describe the nature of the engagement between you and the coach?* There is engagement at multiple levels. The coach understands me well. He asks questions about what I said on previous occasions, which is important. He reminds me of my own aspirations. The engagement has become deeper over time. As the coach has got to know me we have been able to delve into the hinterland. We deal with more than the nuts and bolts. The coach knows how I tick. The engagement has become less day-to-day and much more about me as a leader and as an individual.

Jon has some very revealing comments about the experience at the end of a coaching discussion:

> 'It feels that it has been like a workout. It feels good. I have unburdened. I have had to think. I feel mentally fitter as a consequence. I always go away with two or three things. It is often in the telling that I crystallize my thinking about next steps.'

Some of the key strands from Jon's experience relate to the strength of the personal relationship between Jon and his coach, the quality of the questions, the space given to working through issues and the ability of the coach to understand the client's professional situation and personal make-up.

The potential advantages of coaching for Chief Executives

The potential benefits of coaching for a Chief Executive can be greater than for any other senior leader. Such is the authority a Chief Executive can have that no one else may speak the truth directly to the Chief Executive in such a powerful way. The coach who understands the context in which the Chief Executive operates and has good 'antennae' for how the leader is perceived, by both internal and external stakeholders, can enable the Chief Executive to identify and face up to major challenges that it is imperative to address. 'Speaking truth to power' is one of the important contributions a coach can make for a Chief Executive. The coach has no 'axe to grind', whereas all the other individuals influencing the Chief Executive will have a particular perspective. The coach can stretch and challenge the Chief Executive without risk to their own career.

Coaching can be particularly relevant when a Chief Executive is **new to that post**. Those around them will all have a vested interest and may not be as independent in their thinking and advice as they imagine. Most people will be so keen to make an impact on the Chief Executive that some of the objectivity in their advice may be diminished.

Masoud had just been appointed Chief Executive of an organization with 5000 people. In three coaching sessions before he took up his post, he worked through his vision, his priorities and the values he wanted to embed in his new organization. As a result, he clarified his strategic priorities and had a clear plan for both the first 100 days and the first six months. This enabled him to make an immediate impact, both within the organization and with stakeholders. He described the coaching as 'like talking to yourself in a very structured and disciplined way'. The coaching lasted for eight months, at which point he had set the organization on a clear path: the coaching had served a focused and time-limited purpose.

A coach can help by **stretching the thinking** of a Chief Executive. Even senior members of the organization may not particularly want to disagree with the Chief Executive. All the senior team may have a similar perspective and therefore not always see issues from all the possible angles.

Paul Chandler is the Chief Executive of Traidcraft plc. He talks about the coaching process in the following way:

> 'In the coaching discussion, I feel both comfortable and positively stretched. The coach helps me talk through key issues, with the result being that I see situations from different perspectives and I am able to test out different types of options. As a result of the conversations, I end up with new questions and hypotheses.
>
> 'Sometimes the conversation means that something is brought out of the back of my mind and I am able to make connections with how I have dealt with situations in the past. The process helps me build the more rounded picture. We focus on two or three key issues in each discussion: at the end of each item I feel both stretched and reassured: stretched in terms of the development of new thinking, and reassured in terms of having developed a clarity about a way ahead. It is the external, independent perspective of the coach and the breadth of their experience which helps me test out some of my ideas and crystallize next steps.'

Coaching can help a Chief Executive step up to become **more strategic and less hands on**, allowing their managing directors run their business on a day-to-day basis. Adrian was the CEO of a major international division in the process of merging with another international business, post acquisition, to form a multi-billion-dollar entity. In his original division, he had a typical team of direct reports with whom he ran the business and drove the P&L. He felt stuck, and was struggling to identify how best he could add value.

The coaching breakthrough came when the client let go of his operational mindset and the need to directly run the business. He began to identify with a former plc-CEO who structured his business in a similar way. Emulating his former boss, he learned to leave the subsidiary managing directors to run their businesses day to day but changed his behaviour to one of chairing in style. In this role, he provided the catalyst for his managers to grow the capabilities of their business, drive best practice and think and act strategically, and he identified the linkages externally and across the newly formed group. The coaching discussion had helped identify the scale of the issue, the need for action, the learning from role models and possible ways forward. It had also enabled focused discussions on the progress that had been made.

Coaching can provide an important **sounding board** for a Chief Executive. James is a Chief Executive of a national organization with 92 offices across the country. A lot of the coaching work has been about talking through different approaches to increasing efficiency and effectiveness within the organization. The conversations have helped him work through some of the options in advance of wider discussion with his colleagues. He finds a second opinion so valuable in working through to his own next steps.

Coaching can enable a Chief Executive to **test out specific strategies**. Peter is Chief Executive of an international organization based in Germany. Peter and his coach have been working together for a couple of years. Peter's perspective is:

> *'You don't think you need an executive coach but, when you have one, you realize you do. As a Chief Executive, you need an alter ego to role-play, to test out good ideas and to innovate within a safe environment. You are setting up a virtual world. Good coaching engagement is about quality role-playing and doing a 'what if' analysis. It is road-testing in a safe environment and not a gladiatorial environment. The coach can help you work through what type of position you need to be in. The client is rarely good at everything. The coaching conversations can help build up that greater strength of effective delivery. Leadership is a journey, not a destination. There are ups and downs. The issues it is valuable to work on with a coach are: 'Where am I trying to get to?'; 'Have I got a map?'; 'What tools am I going to need?'. The importance of the coach's job is to support the vision, to help ensure the map reads correctly and to help the client have clarity about where they fit into the bigger map. The engagement with the coach can help the client to stand back. The key role is to ask questions; sometimes they are open and sometimes closed, but they must always be based in a relationship of trust where there is complete openness.'*

Most new Chief Executives are surprised at how their words and actions are magnified both externally and internally. A word out of place and there is a critical headline in the media. What was said as a brief aside internally becomes a new pronouncement about the future direction from the Chief Executive. Becoming a Chief Executive involves a whole new focus on communications. Working through the impact that you want to have in the private confines of a coaching discussion can help prepare both for planned and unplanned moments when a few words are turned into sacred doctrine by the Chief Executive's staff.

A new Chief Executive may find that they are managing for the first time a diverse board of executives and non-executives. Working with a coach who has a parallel experience can provide both practical empathy and sound ideas that can equip the Chief Executive to cope in often complex interrelationships.

At the end of the day, the ultimate responsibility rests with the Chief Executive. In her introduction to the book *Ten Things That Keep CEOs Awake*, Peninah Thomson talks of the varied pressures on the Chief Executive Officer:

> 'They range from the corporate and strategic (how to carve out the time to clarify the vision; retaining a hold on where one is actually taking the business; and managing the board) to the personal and intimate (thinking about how to retain some sort of balance between work and home). Between the two poles of the strategic and the personal are challenges and dilemmas familiar to CEOs. Arguably more operational than strategic, but frequently no less demanding, they are everyday currency in our lives:
>
> - getting the right organizational structure, and deciding whether restructuring is really what is needed;
> - tussling with how best to run a global (and therefore multi-cultural) business;
> - creating appropriate organizational change;
> - acquiring, motivating, developing and keeping talented individuals;
> - the never ending task of communicating with stakeholders (all of them!).'

Because the ultimate responsibility rests with the Chief Executive, prioritising and then prioritizing again is crucial: robust conversation with a coach who can talk on equal terms with the Chief Executive can be an invaluable contributor to success.

Enabling an individual to prepare to become a Chief Executive

Coaching can be productive in enabling an individual to prepare for the step change of becoming a Chief Executive. Coaching can cover the following questions.

- What strengths are going to be most important?
- How do I develop the areas that others are sceptical about?
- What impact do I want to have in the initial weeks?

George went from an investment bank to a utilities company where he was a strong candidate to become the Chief Executive. He had been used to working with very bright people and found it frustrating working with a team who were less able. The dangers were that he would drive himself and everyone else nuts, and he would turn off his direct reports. He was viewed as a bully, but did not accept this perspective. The turning point was when he fully acknowledged the difference between how he communicated at work and how he communicated at home. Without frank discussion with his coach, he would never have accepted the need for change or had that cathartic moment of understanding the difference in his approach at work and at home. The result was that he won the support and respect of the senior team and was appointed Chief Executive.

Meeting reservations from Chief Executives

Except in a few sectors, coaches are seen as a really smart weapon in the armoury. But to some Chief Executives, having a coach gives an appearance of weakness. Because of their role, they are concerned that there should not be any hint that they are not up to the job. Some Chief Executives who have a coach are very reticent to make that fact public but interestingly, when they do, it commands respect and not criticism.

CEOs may be sceptical that the coach will be able to work with them on equal terms. There are trained coaches available who have had very senior level experience: for example, our coaching partnership includes former Chief Executives of FTSE 100 companies. Experienced coaches who have worked closely with Chief Executives can provide the understanding, sensitivity and challenge to work on equal terms with Chief Executives of any organization.

The Chief Executive may see coaching as adding value for others and not for themselves. That may be right, but it is always worth testing the boundary as to how the CEO can raise their performance and what particular skills and competencies they would like to develop further. Good coaching is all about enabling the CEO to continually play 'at the top of their game'. Staff surveys or 360° feedback results are always a good starting point for gauging whether coaching might be relevant at the Chief Executive level.

There may be a suspicion in the mind of a Chief Executive about whether HR has been taken in by the use of psychometrics. Psychometrics might be a turnoff for some Chief Executives, but starting with 360° feedback will almost always catch the interest of a Chief Executive if it means capturing in a clear way the impact they are having and providing scope for them to develop the way they persuade and lead.

While the Chief Executive may support coaching as a way of enabling an individual to take forward their Personal Development Plan, they may feel that coaching is not relevant for them as they do not have a formal Personal Development Plan. Their performance appraisal arrangements may not be very systematic. They may not receive clear advance warning if there are growing perceptions among board members that all is not well. They may not begin to discuss their development needs until it is too late. The absence of systematic feedback can heighten the need for crystallizing priorities through focused dialogue with an executive coach.

Taking forward coaching for Chief Executives

Heather Dawson, in her chapter *Developing Bifocal Vision* in the book *Ten Things That Keep CEOs Awake*, talks of the main responsibility of a Chief Executive being to develop a clear vision of where he or she wishes to take the company. She observes from her coaching practice that CEOs have difficulty doing this because they have insufficient unallocated time to think and reflect; because retaining clarity for the short and long term is a rare skill; and because they are expected to have all the answers. She sees three key areas: balancing short and long term; knowing where to be 'hands off' and 'hands on'; and creating a strong senior executive group. A key theme for Heather is enabling the CEO to be clear where they add most value and how to manage the senior team within that perspective.

In the same book, Elspeth May, in her chapter *Creating Time to Maximise CEO Impact*, talks of important self-protection measures for CEOs, covering buffering your self-confidence, making sure you have a good support mechanism, using your friends and family, and find friends in your working world. At the heart of Elspeth's coaching work with CEOs is tackling these questions:

- What can I, and only I, do for this organization?
- To whom can I delegate the rest?
- How can I create more thinking time?
- Do I need an effective blocking PA?
- How do I move from professional survival to personal fulfilment?
- How can I control the information flow to what I need, when I need it?
- How can I protect myself from media-induced stress?
- How can I create time for maintaining my own health and wellbeing?

Reflecting on these issues demonstrates the potential benefit that a Chief Executive can gain from engagement with a coach. If it helps them to be clear what they, and nobody else, can do for the benefit of their organization, then it will have served its purpose in focusing the value-added of the Chief Executive within:

- my *role* (how I am going to work);
- my *agenda* (what I am going to work on); and
- my *team* (who I am going to work with).

Chapter 8:

Different Contexts where Coaching Can Make a Significant Difference

This chapter addresses the different contexts where individual coaching can make a significant difference. It starts from the importance of coach and client having a clear sense of strategic priorities, with the client willing to address challenges in a focused way. Specific contexts it addresses are:

- becoming a board member;
- high potential individuals;
- new-to-role;
- making the most of secondments;
- approaching promotion;
- when a specific issue is holding an individual back;
- when performance needs to be improved;
- when an individual should move on;
- addressing gender difference;
- coaching for minority groups;
- increasing personal impact before an interview;
- living through turbulence; and
- finding your future.

A key theme is the way coaching engagements make a significant difference in terms of an individual's knowledge, authority, influence, presence, success and gravitas.

Individuals are unique, and as a result have distinct combinations of skills, knowledge, abilities, experiences, environment, values, aspirations and behaviours. The agendas that they bring to coaching are varied, but each person will have two or three priority agenda items gleaned from a focused agenda-setting meeting with a coach. This chapter looks at a selection of the many possible agendas and how some key overall themes are relevant whatever the agenda.

Overriding themes

In each of these examples, the conversations must be rooted in what is most important. Coach and client must have a clear sense of priorities. They need to be strategic about what they discuss and clear about their objectives, and need to avoid getting into the dross too much. It is important that they stand above the detail. This may mean tackling specific issues but always in a wider context. Engagement on a particular issue has to be rooted in clarity about what the coaching is there for.

Staying strategic covers both the topics and the behaviours. The client needs to address challenges and behaviours in a way that is bold, measured, pragmatic and thought through. That relates just as much to addressing policy and operational aspects as it does to moving on to a new level of confidence and personal impact.

In any of the situations described within this chapter, the client should develop knowledge, authority, influence, presence, success, gravitas and self-awareness as a result of the coaching engagement (see Fig. 8.1).

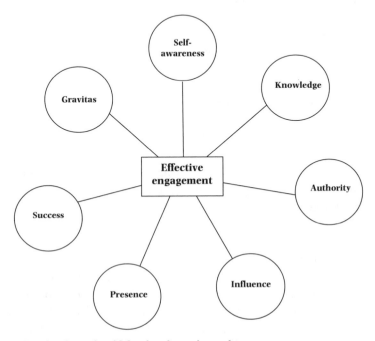

Fig. 8.1 What the client should develop through coaching

These dimensions are:

- **knowledge:** clarity about what facts and information are most important in measuring progress, assessing risks and moving ahead;
- **authority:** developing clarity about next steps, stage-managing discussions well and building respect;
- **influence:** developing the ability to understand, influence and keep the trust and support of champions, stakeholders and staff;
- **presence:** being able to influence the pace and stage-manage discussions and next steps, knowing when to intervene and when to hold back;
- **success:** clarity about what success is in terms of it being realistic and stretching with a strong emphasis on shared success;
- **gravitas:** being listened to and making things happen through others; and
- **self-awareness:** understanding the pattern of your own reactions and not being thrown by difficult or unexpected situations.

Becoming a board member

Becoming a board member is a major step change. Situations where coaching has been particularly applicable have included:

- a new board member who was very entrepreneurial and needed to become much more focused as a board member;
- a Finance Director who drove people very hard who was moving into a policy role and needed to adjust his style; and
- an individual who was great working with key players in the City but couldn't manage or inspire and needed to develop his leadership skills.

For each of these people the coaching engagement was about helping an individual be very clear what strengths had brought them to their particular position in the organization, the context that they were now working in and how they needed to adjust their priorities and approach.

James was a newly appointed board member of an international communications organization. What had got him to this position (European CEO) was a career coming up the marketing function in different businesses within the sector. What had also got him there was an inordinate grasp of tremendous amounts of detail and an ability to work twelve-hour days (and thus meet both American and Asiapac telephone demands).

What he failed to grasp was the whole new paradigm shift he required. He now had to share responsibility for the worldwide organization's health as well as direct the European piece. This led him to a requirement to understand much more at a higher level and also have an informal view (relying on others). He recognized the need, but found great difficulty adjusting his task schedule to the expectations of those around him.

Becoming a board member can require a step-change in a range of different areas. It means adjusting to the following type of step-changes and becoming more:

- **strategic** – being clear about the bigger picture and where the business needs to go with a clear understanding of the change in context;
- **representational** – building stakeholder relationships at the right level and seeing how mutual interest and partnerships can be developed;
- **corporate** – recognising that what matters is the success of the whole business and not just the individual's area; it is interlinking effectively the ways in which how different strands of the organization will ensure or diminish corporate success;
- **accountable** – demonstrating accountability for the success of the whole business where success in an individual's area without success across the organization as a whole is not an adequate expression of personal accountability;
- **visible** – giving a conscious lead through content and behaviour to the rest of the organization, recognizing that individual commitment and behaviour at senior levels is a touchstone right through an organization;
- **thinly stretched** – recognizing that the individual's value-added comes through understanding the wider context and likely reactions rather than detailed knowledge of particular areas. Adjusting to living with more minimal information is an essential part of moving up to board level; and
- **time-efficient** – much of what a board member does is determined by areas on which they want to focus. It may be devoting a considerable time to growing others and mentoring people with potential in the organization.

A board member has to do a balancing act with their energies and time. The framework above can help an individual develop greater clarity about their role, their priorities and the impact that they want to have. Engagement with a coach at this level can then be balanced with addressing specific issues. The best of coaching engagement may well be moving interchangeably between these bigger issues and specific problems.

Coaching for non-executive board members can be particularly relevant in helping an individual move from the executive type responsibilities they might have had before into the very different role of a non-executive board member. It is about helping an individual be clear about where they can best add value. It is helping someone stand back and not do the executives' jobs for them.

High-potential individuals

Hilary Douglas, who has led on HR and Change Management in six government organizations, describes the value of coaching for high-potential people in this way:

> 'Part of the crucial preparation for them is thinking hard about leadership style and building a wider range of tools into their kitbag. Coaching can enable them to develop their skills and practise them in a safe environment where the coach can challenge them hard so that they embed their learning effectively.'

A marketing director talking of his immediate high-potential successors expressed his view of where coaching can help:

> 'They [the high-potential individuals] need to make the transition from being sent on missions to defending what the missions are; from pleasing the bosses to challenging the status quo.'

Noel Hadden at Deutsche Bank sees high-potential staff as particularly benefiting from coaching when semi-structured 360° interviews are used as part of it. It is all about 'holding a mirror to them and then helping them fulfil their high potential'.

For high-potential individuals in any type of organization, coaching needs to be based on a commitment from both the individual and the organization in terms of time and expectations. The high-potential individual must be in a frame of mind where, irrespective of their natural gifts, they want to learn in new and sometimes demanding ways. Charlie Massey is on the UK Cabinet Office High Potential Development Scheme, designed for people with the potential to reach the highest levels of the UK Civil Service. As soon as he went on the scheme, he began to work with a coach, and this has continued as he has moved into a significantly more demanding role. Because Charlie is task-focused, he can find it difficult to focus on personal development. Charlie says of the coaching:

'It forces me to focus on my own personal development. My coach keeps holding me to account. He makes me reflect on the things I have done and how I might do things differently. I come away from our coaching conversations with learning firmly embedded. The opportunity to reflect and work things through in conversation in a different environment is so valuable.'

New-to-role

A buyer of coaching in a high-profile national organization talks of coaching being particularly powerful in getting people up to speed quickly if they are new to their role. Crucial outcomes from the coaching will be: the coachee does an effective job right from the start; the learning curve is steep and efficient; priorities are defined and developed effectively; crucial relationships are built quickly; and the individual is able to make an impact quickly within the organization, is motivated to stay and learns how best to work within the culture. In addition, the individual maintains their drive and personal equilibrium and continues to develop their competences.

To be effective, the coach needs to receive in advance a clear brief from the organization about the nature of the job, the expectations of the postholder and the feedback arrangements that will operate.

Prior to taking up the role, or immediately on starting in the role, the coach and the individual should ideally together consider issues like these.

- What outcomes does the organization want in your area of responsibility, at the end of three months and at the one-year point?
- What does the organization particularly want you to contribute to the delivery of these outcomes?
- What are your personal targets, for the end of three months and the end of year one?
- What are your priority areas for the first month?
- What are your key strengths and how are you going to use them?
- What excites you most about this new role?
- What are you most apprehensive about in this new role? What skills do you need to develop?
- How are you going to manage your time? How are you going to recharge your batteries?

Key strands in the coaching conversations in terms of personal targets and priority areas might include: what progress you are making in mastering the issues; how you are going to manage relationships upwards, with your peers and with your direct reports; how you are going to ensure your maximum visibility within your organization; what values are most important to you; and how do you want to ensure those values are embedded in your organization.

Progress meetings between coach and client could be covering aspects like these.

- What is the progress on delivering the outcomes?
- Are you making the progress you want in mastering the issues? Is your progress matching your priorities established when taking on this job?
- How are the relationships working (a) upwards (b) with peers (c) with direct reports?
- Are you able to live your values? What are you finding most difficult?
- What is keeping you awake at night? How are you keeping space for structured reflection?
- What feedback are you receiving from colleagues?

At the end of each meeting, there would need to be agreement on the issues to be worked on and the topics that should be discussed at the next meeting, recognizing that they might need to change by the start of the next meeting.

At the end of the coaching programme, there needs to be an agreed understanding of progress made and a commitment by the client to next steps.

Making the most of secondments

A similar approach to working with people new to their role can be used with individuals on secondment. Secondments between different organizations are increasingly seen as a means of widening an individual's experience and understanding, but there is often resistance to secondments because of the time taken to build up expertise. Coaching can play an important part in helping to ensure that secondments are successful, from the perspectives of the organizations and the individual.

The priority areas for coaching might include: maximizing the benefits for the receiving organization of the individual's experience; embedding effective learning from the secondment; and preparing effectively for the next role after secondment.

Approaching promotion

Many organizations talk of the relatively limited availability of talent and the importance of developing people effectively for promotion. Coaching can make a focused contribution where it is clear what the business needs are and what competences an individual needs to develop in order to be a strong candidate for promotion. Some organizations have found it helpful to put a structure around this type of development. An approach that is being used in a national organization applies the following steps:

Initially:
- The client either sends the coach in advance or comes to the first coaching meeting armed with any 360° written feedback data and their most recent performance assessment;
- The coach and client agree on:
  - the key issues to be worked on (normally 3–5); and
  - the outcomes sought in these 3 areas.
- These issues and outcomes sought are agreed with the line manager;

After five sessions:
  - the client does a brief self-assessment of progress on the key issues and outcomes set at the start;
  - the line manager does a brief assessment of progress on key issues and outcomes set out at the start which is shared with the coach and the client; and
  - the views of direct reports are sought on the progress so far via a short written form which is returned to the coach.

In the sixth session:
- The coach and client agree next steps in light of the feedback; and
- A short note goes to the Personnel Training Department copied to the line manager which has been agreed by the coach and client about:
  - the issues worked on;
  - the outcomes sought; and
  - progress on the outcomes, including a short summary of the views of direct reports.

There is no major formula: the example above is purely illustrative. Any approach to preparing people for promotion needs to fit the circumstances of individual organizations. But there are common themes covering realism about an individual's potential, stretch covering the opportunities they are put into and feedback covering the honesty and supportiveness of what is felt about their progress. Overlaying these strands is the need for the individual to build a reputation. It is as an individual builds their own reputation for delivery with senior people that they strengthen the likelihood of promotion.

When a specific issue is holding an individual back

Hilary Douglas comments that a person who is not performing to their full potential will ideally be coached by their line manager and peers but sometimes an external professional is needed to make the difference – and possibly to help the line manager to see what is needed.

Where a specific issue is holding an individual back the crucial outcome is that significant progress is made addressing the issue. It is about enabling someone to look at the effect of their behaviours objectively. The following illustrative approach is based on the member of staff being clear at the start about the issue they want to address and why they want to address it. The first step is to identify how much is an issue that is real and how much it's perceived. Do the line manager and other key players share the same view as the individual? There needs to be a shared understanding about the extent to which the individual believes it is redeemable and what steps have been tried in the past.

The initial coaching could consider:

- precisely what the issue is and whether the problem is a shared perception;
- what has been tried before and what the results of those steps were;
- what are the outcomes an individual particularly wants to achieve and what are the milestones on the way:
- what are initial steps the individual would like to take;
  - the extent to which this is an issue about competence or confidence; and
  - what would increase the individual's confidence in being able to take those steps:
- how the individual can best create the time to work on this issue; and
- how the individual will know that they are making progress: whether or not there are one or two peers with whom the individual has a trust relationship with whom they can work on the issue and receive honest feedback.

At progress meetings some of the following issues might helpfully be considered:

- does the individual believe they are making good progress and what is the feedback from others on their progress?
- what steps are they finding particularly helpful in working on this issue and what aspects are they finding particularly difficult?
- how can the coach and client best work through some of the issues in a way which reinforces this new approach to addressing this issue?
- how can the individual reinforce the success that they are experiencing – do they need a campaign to persuade others that they are now fully effective in this area?

At the end of the coaching there needs to be an agreed understanding of progress made and a commitment by the client to next steps.

Whatever approach is taken it needs to be set within the context of the themes at the start of the chapter. Is what is holding an individual back related to knowledge, limited authority, low influence, inadequate presence, lack of clarity about success, low self-awareness or the wrong sort of gravitas? The right sort of engagement will need to build on one or more of these key themes if the client is going to make the necessary step change in their performance.

As an example Christophe was a French national within banking who was open to coaching because a promotion to Managing Director was at stake. The issue presented by the HR Director was that, 'Although a fantastic performer, his style is of some concern and his superiors say he is too emotional. As such he is either looking at the world as wonderful or things are at the end of the world. His 360° feedback says he needs to be a bit calmer and to manage his highly strung style.'

The first two meetings with his coach established the key item – talking exceptionally quickly in English with a French accent. From the reactions he perceived he got in meetings when he practised talking more slowly and deliberately, he began to be less frustrated and more engaged with others. This 'calmed' him. While there were many other agenda items for coaching, this specific issue was the priority and was addressed over three months through coaching.

Performance needs to be improved

There may be specific areas in an individual's performance that are not satisfactory where a step change in improved performance is needed. Outcomes from coaching in these situations might include a clear pathway of training and development, focused aspirations, raised confidence in the sharpness of an individual's contribution, realism and honesty about next steps and more effective personal contributions.

A shared understanding about the area where improvement is needed and the causes of the need for improvement are necessary. These might include inexperience, a specific training requirement, the need for a wider perspective to deliver the job effectively and the necessity of new challenge in the current job.

Some of the ingredients of the coaching relationship could include a clear initial brief from personnel about the background and expectations, discussion with the current line manager about the individual in their current role, and the preparation of an action plan by the individual which is discussed with the coach before it is finalized. The coaching discussions would be based on the plan and help with progress towards the delivery of the necessary changes.

The nature of the coaching relationship will depend on the circumstances of the individual. Possible elements of coaching might be:

(a) **For an inexperienced individual:** the coaching could include: an honest agreed assessment with the coachee about what further experience is to be gained and the training to be undergone, clarity about what the individual is expected to deliver over the forthcoming months, clarifying the particular 'value added' the individual is due to bring, identifying the means of gaining wider experience, defining how that learning is to be internalized and being clear what the feedback arrangements about progress are. Agreed milestones would need to be established to help assess that progress is being made through the coaching sessions.

(b) **For an individual needing a new challenge** there would need to be clarity about the skills which have developed in the current job, what skills and experience the organization wants the individual to develop over the next months and the extent that this is going to be achieved by a new challenge within the existing role or through a new job. Agreed milestones in developing and taking forward the new challenge would be needed.

(c) **For an individual who needs to develop their performance in particular competences** the process would need to involve identifying the competences where progress is needed, clarifying what it is the individual finds difficult and the use of focused good practice tools to help work with an individual to develop the competences (e.g. difference between leadership and management, delegation skills, time management). Effective engagement between coach, client and line manager will be important throughout this process including clear feedback about how well an individual is doing.

An individual who should move on

Coaching can play an important role where an individual has been doing a job for a number of years and needs to move on either because they are becoming a little stale or they need to be stretched in new areas. This is particularly relevant where organizations have a policy of individuals normally staying in post for a maximum of four or five years. Crucial outcomes from the coaching in these circumstances are greater clarity about next steps for the individual, Increased confidence in pursuing options, greater self-awareness about the perception of others and a fresh approach based on thinking outside the box.

Where the individual and organization are in broad agreement about next steps the coaching could cover such steps as how best to prepare for these next steps including building on strengths and the development needs that can be worked on in coaching or training (e.g. delegation skills, time management, managing change, building effective relationships, negotiation). The coaching could include preparing a clear CV and preparing for an interview or considering what the networks and experience to build up are.

Where the individual and organization are less clear about next steps the coaching would involve some lateral thinking about options such as an individual identifying four types of options of which say two are within the organization and two in other organizations. For each option the individual 'sits' in each role, describes the activities being done, the emotions being felt, the pleasures and the stresses. The coach relates to the individual as if the individual was in the role. The skilled coach will build on this approach to test out a variety of options.

Often the key starting point is building up an individual's confidence in their knowledge, authority, influence, presence, gravitas and self-awareness as an essential part of helping someone to move on in a positive and expectant frame of mind.

Coaching to address gender difference

The dynamic of gender difference has been discussed in the book 'A woman's place is in the Boardroom' by Peninah Thomson, Jacey Graham and Tom Lloyd (2005). In it the authors describe an innovative programme – the

FTSE 100 Cross-Company Mentoring Programme – in which a number of high potential women in roles just below the Board are being mentored by FTSE 100 company Chairmen. As the book states in its conclusion (page 206/7):

> 'We have argued in this book that men and women lead differently, that, for historical reasons, business organizations bear the imprints of masculine values, norms and patterns of behaviour and that, as a result of this, the cultures of companies frequently don't 'fit' women, particularly at senior levels where women remain thin on the ground. Two consequences arise from this. The few women who do manage to reach the top of large companies often feel abraded by the cultures they find there, and women just below the board, who look up at the top of the management pyramid, often decide not to participate, because the price they will have to pay seems too great... A new compact between the sexes must be reached about how our large companies are organised, managed and led, that makes them better adapted to and more welcoming for women.'

Coaching which enables women to take a leading role in organizations will take account of both individual and organizational needs. The positive effect on the quality of decision making at senior levels following from the promotion of able women is testament to the value of enabling women to fulfil their potential with the assistance of coaching.

Coaching for minority groups

Coaching can play a key role for those in minority groups where confidence can be a major issue holding an individual back. A number of organizations have introduced programmes which have focused on the particular needs of women, the disabled or members of ethnic minorities.

As an example the Pathways programme provides leadership development for members of ethnic minorities who are regarded by UK Government Departments as having high potential. The programme is a mixture of training days, learning sets and one-to-one coaching. The programme also involves project work which aims to be at the cutting edge of leadership thinking within Government Departments. The coaching has been a valuable ingredient in reinforcing learning from training days. The benefits of the coaching have been principally increased confidence in dealing with different situations, a greater focus in the use of time and energy and the development of a more targeted set of aspirations.

Overcoming any sense of disadvantage about being part of a minority group depends on an individual's sense of drive and commitment. The biggest impact invariably comes from enabling members of ethnic minorities to fulfil their potential for leadership through a combination of courage and pragmatism.

Increasing personal impact before an interview

The starting point for coaching may be preparing somebody for an interview. Enabling an individual to be clear on their unique selling points and how they are going to communicate them will always catch the imagination of somebody preparing for an interview. They are the same principles that apply in terms of their personal impact in a new job or any new situation.

Enabling individuals to have a couple of coaching sessions prior to a major interview is not discriminatory. It is about enabling somebody to demonstrate their competencies to the best possible effect. An ideal arrangement is for all the candidates for a particular post to have the opportunity for some focused interview training which will ensure a level playing field and enable the interviewers to have a complete picture of the strengths of the candidates.

Key features of effective coaching for personal impact in an interview are: clarity about the adjectives an individual wants people to use to describe them; the evidence to be used to demonstrate that these are the right adjectives; understanding the perspective of the interviewers; setting out clearly their unique selling points and what they have achieved. The panel will want to be persuaded that the good candidate can move the panel's thinking on and is someone they would like to have on their team.

Living through turbulence

Coaching can have a valuable role when an organization is going through turbulence. Any organization which is in the media spotlight is not going to be the most comfortable place in which to work. Those in senior roles in any organization in the spotlight will rise to the challenge through demonstrating commitment and determination. But the pressures can be relentless and take their toll.

Those affected by major external controversies are both the individuals directly affected who have policy or operational responsibility, those within the same part of the organization who feel some of the fall-out and others elsewhere in the organization who are feeling that a risk they are dealing with could be the next one to blow.

Time spent with an external coach for those directly affected can provide the space to think through some of the issues and clarify priorities, put the current controversy in a wider context, say the unspoken things and provide an appropriate context for the expression of emotions such as anger or feeling let down. The coaching engagement can reinforce self-confidence about taking tough decisions that are necessary, provide a breathing space to recharge energy levels and enable an independent person to help somebody recognize whether they are being entirely rational or not.

Coaching conversations with those less immediately involved but who feel the turbulence might affect them next can enable them to keep their cool in focusing on their own priorities, be rational in looking at risks, prioritise effectively and have the courage to be clear where major problems can occur.

The task of coaching in these situations is to help people cope with any waves from the impact of controversy, enabling them to maintain their confidence and coolness, keeping a strong focus on delivery. Time with an external coach in these circumstances is complementary to mentoring by somebody senior within the organization.

Finding your future

Coaching can play an important part in enabling somebody to think constructively about the future direction of their career or of how they want to spend their time and energy over forthcoming years. Coaching work that enables somebody to look ahead constructively can be particularly pertinent at crucial stages in life such as turning 40, turning 50 or reaching an age where retirement is beginning to come into view. Effective coaching conversations in these situations are about living your values, reflecting on what will give you greatest joy in the future, how your skills and understanding can be used to best effect for the benefit of others, how you are going to keep fresh and energized, what the new challenges which you would like to take on are, and what are the next phases of life you would like to go through.

The 55-year-old who might be tempted to coast to retirement can be re-energized through looking ahead and continuing to develop their skills and networks so that they can move smoothly into another world post retirement.

When individuals become bored, frustrated or downhearted four key steps are:

- **looking at starting points** which helps you establish where you are now through looking at frustrations, failure, fears and fortitude;
- **taking stock** which enables you to reflect on the various influences upon you, especially family, friends, and finance as well as looking at what the fundamentals are;
- **looking forward** which helps you establish the prerequisites for next steps which might include forgiveness, following fascinations, engaging with the freedom that is available and using fasting or self-denial; and
- **moving on** which involves encouraging you to develop foresight, have a clear focus and bring a sense of fun as you look to achieve a greater degree of fulfilment in the next phase of your life.*

Conclusion

This chapter has illustrated a range of different situations where individual coaching can have a significant impact. The crucial questions for an organization to ask are:

- With what groups and individuals is targeted investment of coaching likely to have the biggest impact?
- What is the relative focus that we want to put on short term and long terms needs?
- Where is the ripple effect of coaching going to be most effective?
- For the different groups, what is going to be the best combination of one-to-one coaching and team coaching?

The choice of coaching approaches needs to be set firmly within the organization's view about what are the most important themes. In particular how the coaching engagements make a significant difference in terms of an individual's knowledge, authority, influence, presence, success and gravitas needs to be established..

---

* Peter Shaw sets out this framework in detail in his book *Finding your Future: the second time around* (Darton, Longman and Todd, 2006)

Chapter 9:

The Difference Between Coaching and Mentoring

This chapter looks at the difference between coaching and mentoring, which are complementary activities that sometimes overlap in implementation. The chapter addresses:

- who is a coach and who is a mentor;
- how and from whom do we learn;
- the importance of relationships in learning; and
- examples of mentoring arrangements.

The key theme is for an individual to maximize the learning they receive from engagement with their line manager, their mentor or mentors and a coach, using each engagement to complement and reinforce the learning from other sources.

An external business coach is often confused with an external business mentor. The former may have no expertise of the client's business sector and engages in coaching the individual in the situation he or she is in. The business mentor is an experienced executive from the same or similar business who has greater direct experience of the situation of the client and can work with them through the content of the situation. In this chapter we shall concern ourselves primarily with the external coach and the internal mentor.

Who is a coach and who is a mentor?

Who is a coach and who is a mentor (Fig. 9.1)? Four cameos to help our understanding:

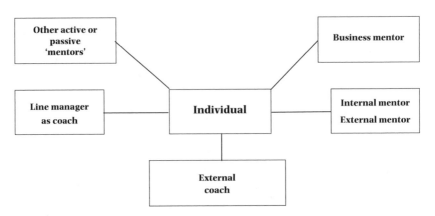

Fig. 9.1 Different types of mentor

- Karren Brady is Birmingham City Football Club's managing director. She was sales and marketing manager to David Sullivan before he bought Birmingham City from receivership in 1993. She says

  'All successful people need someone to rely on as a mentor. We work side by side, and he develops the bits of me that needed attention, enhancing my ability to sell. I was enthusiastic and had the ability to be on top of things fast, never missing a selling opportunity. You can't learn these skills on a course. He is my boss and my best friend. We speak fifteen times a day, and I can't envisage not working for him. We are on the same wavelength and I guess I am a product of his business ability.'
  (*Sunday Times*, 11 May 1997. Reproduced by permission of the *Sunday Times*. Kindly supplied by NI Syndication.)

- A man decided to set up his own business. He was a good cook and had a caravan so he set up a sign at the end of a lay-by and began to sell hot dogs. It was a good road with lots of traffic and he did very well. So well that it became too big for him and he thought about bringing someone else in. His son had just finished at business school and said to his dad that there was a recession on. 'You will have to cut back to be ready for the upturn when it comes,' said the son and so his dad took down the sign at the end of the lay-by and concentrated on existing customers as a precaution. Sales began to go down and he said to his son: 'You were right – there is a recession!'

- Sir Christopher Harding was the chairman of United Utilities, Legal & General, and BNFL. Following his tragic early death a leadership programme was set up in his name. It described Christopher Harding as an extraordinary business leader. His entrepreneurial spirit, combined with his commitment to help people develop their full potential and to enable organizations to face their social and environmental responsibilities, was universally recognized as a model of inspirational leadership.

- In Homer's Odyssey, Telemachus is attempting to find his father Odysseus who has been trying for years to get home to Greece from the Trojan Wars. He wants to speak to Nestor who might know where his father is: he says to his trusted advisor, 'Mentor, how am I to go up to the great man? How shall I greet him? Remember that I have had no practice in making speeches; and a young man may well hesitate to cross-examine one so much his senior'. The response was, 'Telemachus, where your native wit fails, heaven will inspire you. It is not for nothing that the Gods have watched your progress ever since your birth ...' So Telemachus, inspired by Mentor, now plucked up the courage to make him a spirited reply ...

Reflections from these cameos are:

- Is David Sullivan a coach or a mentor?
- Is the business school son an upward mentor or a consultant?
- Is Sir Christopher Harding a mentor or a role model?
- Is Nestor a mentor or a trusted counsellor?

The difficulty with these questions is that at one level the words and language get in the way of discovering the truth about what can be learned from the stories. At another level, is the question of the difference between coaching and mentoring just a version of the philosophical debate about how many angels can dance on a pinhead? We need to dig deeper.

What is underlying all the stories is that all four are in some way engaged in helping people to enhance their effectiveness in their place of work, to learn more effectively and to increase their capacity for learning. One of the key learnings for the hot dog salesman is to always seek a second opinion and question the first one!

How and from whom do we learn

A major international energy company wrote the following in an internal document:

> 'We will be an international employer of first choice, together creating a safe, healthy and creative environment where we can all be proud to

work, and where we can develop and grow collectively and individually.'

Like many organizations, this company had put in place various measures to ensure that it achieves 'breakthrough performance, namely providing learning and development opportunities, unleashing talent and contribution at all levels and, through continuous learning, the stimulation of learning at all levels.'

In the current economic climate, this company has placed a lot of emphasis on developing a setting within which the individual is encouraged to draw on their own resources and to take responsibility for the work that they do. With an increasing emphasis on self improvement, individuals are managing the organizational and personal implications of pursuing their own 'big ticket items'. Empowerment is the order of the day.

In an ideal world the individual is enabled to learn more effectively and to increase their capacity for learning. The world is not ideal and people need help and support but nobody can take responsibility for another person's learning. People bring their own interpretations to the work that they do, to the teams within which they work and to the organizational culture within which it is all set. No teacher, trainer, coach, counsellor, consultant, mentor or manager (let's call all these generically the 'other person') can simply get people to sit still while they, the experts, pour 'knowledge' in. We work out what situations mean to us and what action we are going to take, and that is the process which needs to be encouraged if people are really going to learn to operate more effectively at the individual, team, and organizational level.

The role of the other person is to take part with the individual in that process of learning. It is not instruction, it is also not simply creating the conditions within which the individual feels free to learn for themselves. The other person brings his or her experience to the table too, and by conversation and by encouraging the individual to reflect, to explore, to question, he or she helps that person's learning. Depending upon the circumstances and the setting, the focus may be firmly located in the here-and-now or it may include a longer term look encompassing work and lifestyle.

In our experience, three people are key in enabling individuals to gain maximum learning. There will be typical areas of focus as highlighted below, but they are not exclusively the domain of each role person – there will be cross-over.

Firstly **line managers themselves** are increasingly being encouraged to take on a development role. This means the manager acting less in a directive capacity and more as an 'enabler of learning'. There is a growing practice of talking about the manager as coach. This draws consciously on the sporting metaphor where what the manager is good at is enhancing sporting ability in others. Typical areas of focus will be: clarity about role and job expectations, clarity about what is success, regular feedback, establishing an atmosphere in the local job setting for learning and effective performance and giving regular personal feedback.

Secondly there is someone **in the same organization but not in the direct management line**. Often this is someone older, more senior or someone who has been that way before. The practice is to refer to this person as a '**mentor**', an expert about the local environment. The distinction between the mentor and the manager as coach is that the former has no line management responsibility. Key areas here could be: providing corporate direction, helping thinking and planning on overall career development, providing a source of knowledge of the organization, its political climate and the organizational politics, acting as a sounding board for ideas and being a role model. This role of mentor can be undertaken by someone external or internal to the organization.

Thirdly there is the **external resource**. This is particularly appropriate for people in senior positions for whom a wider perspective is important. For simplicity's sake we call this person a '**business coach**' and the practice in which they engage 'business coaching'. The coach has experience that extends well beyond the limits of the individual's own organization. Typically it is someone operating professionally as an 'enabler of learning' full-time. Key focus areas in this instance are: coaching individuals to learn developing capabilities, asking questions to challenge as well as to help individuals understand their own thought processes, providing an external independent ear and objective view, working through the organisation's demands in terms of career, performance and personal circumstances, working on problems and learning together in action learning mode and helping to appreciate personal best and effective performance.

The 'business coach would actively work to outcomes and objectives in the coaching with the client. The 'mentor' would be more inclined to advise generally on key areas identified.

The manager, the mentor and the coach have particular roles. For any individual executive these roles are three of many influences in their personal and working lives. Figure 9.2 shows some of these wider influences against a continuum of how active or passive their involvement with the individual is.

The continuum involvement can equally stretch from being directive and guiding the individual about what they should do, to being non-directive in enabling the individual solve their problems. The influences might be at different positions or points on the continuum but each one can have a distinct role to play.

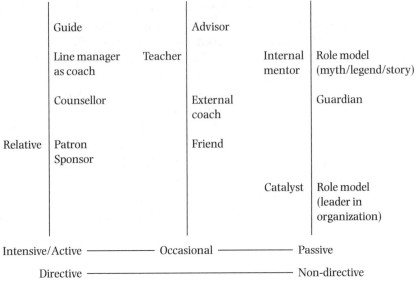

Fig. 9.2 The wider influences on an executive director vs activity/passivity

The importance of relationships in learning

More than one influencer is likely to be involved with an individual at any one point in time. In the Pathways Programme and the CB Richard Ellis programme (outlined below), the line manager, mentor and coach are active influencers at the same time.

At their essence, coaching and mentoring are forms of relationship and not procedures or programmes or activities. John Adair's book *How to Grow Leaders* (2005) highlights the apprenticeship method as a fundamental example of a learning process through a relationship:

> 'A would-be practitioner articles himself formally or informally to a master-craftsman, and in return for a very modest wage he worked alongside the master. The master's role was to show by example, but also to instruct, explain or teach as well ... If you look carefully at the careers of outstanding leaders in any field, you usually find that they learned most about leadership not from courses or books, but by serving their apprenticeship with a master-leader. You should not assume that leadership mentors are always senior to you in the hierarchy ...'

Relationships are crucial to learning. Young children in the Roman world would learn the value of two key attitudes from their father – firstly **pietas** which was a devotion to the Gods, the state and also to the family which are essentially external attributes; secondly **gravitas** which involved having a sense of gravity, dignity and responsibility which are essentially internal attributes. In this ancient world both of these attitudes were equally important and would be appealed to when any new different situation arose.

Focused personal attention is a key to the development of individuals. Talking with the other person can unlock information or resources already within you which you had not realized were present until that moment. It mirrors Bunyan's *Pilgrim's Progress* where Christian is held captive in a dungeon by Giant Despair and a conversation with Hopeful leads to the realization that he has the Key of Promise on him which he had forgotten about. He uses it and goes free.

When Robin was working at Shell there were MADECs (Management Development Courses), AMSGs (Advanced Management Study Groups) and others where information had been pumped into him. The real learning however came from the relationships built up in those courses, in the evenings and afterwards where peers, colleagues and bosses had become his co-workers in learning – the 'other persons' of significance.

For the line manager, mentor or coach key considerations are:

1   *The proximity to the workplace* – the mentor might know the place of work because they work in it, while the coach can come from outside or inside (line manager) the organization, and the line manager will be from inside the organization.
2   *The timeframes involved* – a mentor may well work on a longer timeframe with the individual because often the relationship is geared to developing an individual's career. The line manager will be concerned more with the immediate and short term. The external coach will be concerned more with the medium to long term, but could also be involved in the short issue dimension.
3   *Questioning* – the line manager, mentor and external coach all need to learn the art of asking the right questions. The Socratic approach is fundamental in this. Socrates was always prepared to discuss and make people think. His method of achieving knowledge was through the process of question and answers, which lead to precise definition and understanding.

Examples of mentoring arrangements

So how does mentoring actually work alongside coaching? Three examples can illustrate this:

1   *FTSE100 Cross Company Mentoring.* Peninah Thomson, assisted by
    Jacey Graham and on behalf of the UK Consortium Group, Women
    Directors on Boards, has established a FTSE100 cross company men-
    toring programme. This helps women mentees to manage their careers
    so that they can attain a non-executive director or an executive director
    role. It does so by linking FTSE100 chairmen as mentors to the women
    mentees. Some of the women are also being coached in parallel.

2   *Cabinet Office – Pathways.* This is a programme which ran from 2001 to
    2006 for groups of 20 ethnic minority next generation leaders of the
    Senior Civil Service (SCS). The central feature is the personal develop-
    ment plan which is drawn up by the individual with their line man-
    ager. The coach works with the individual to make the plan specific and
    focused and then coaches in particular areas. The trained mentor is
    another member of the SCS from another Department who mentors
    the individual in any aspect of leadership but especially their career
    direction and addressing enablers or blockers to that.

3   *CB Richard Ellis.* The senior management of CB Richard Ellis aims to
    support current and future leaders in the business in developing their
    range of skills and approaches, their understanding of the commer-
    cial realities and business activities of CBRE and their leadership and
    management capability. Selected members of management have been
    trained in mentoring and have been matched with mentees to work to-
    gether over a one year period. The mentors act in many different roles,
    e.g. role model of leadership, expert source of professional knowledge
    and sounding boards for ideas, etc. Some of the mentors are also being
    coached in their own management roles at the same time and in their
    mentoring skills.

Conclusion

There is both a role for mentoring and a role for coaching. Terminology can
get in the way but the roles of line manager, internal mentor and external
coach are distinct and complimentary. The key is to be an expert at asking
questions and not to act like the singer in *The Sound of Music* who says 'You
are 16 going on 17 ... you need someone older and wiser, telling you what to
do!' As Steve Fairbairn said in his 1926 *Rowing Notes*: 'One wants to coach
a man to coach himself.'

Chapter 10:

Meeting Business Priorities

This chapter focuses on meeting business priorities. It is concerned with enabling individuals to achieve alignment in meeting a range of different business priorities. The chapter looks at:
- 'the Theatre of Business';
- reflecting on coping with changing business priorities by using an illustration;
- focusing coaching to address business priorities within the sponsoring organization, the coaching firm and within the coaching process; and
- evaluating of coaching work.

Success is dependent on alignment in helping clients meet business priorities, with effective evaluation of whether their business priorities are being met.

Clients will have both individual objectives and organizational objectives to achieve. Their individual objectives will fall into one of three categories: those that are work-related (e.g. sales figures, strategic review, recruiting new board members, acquiring new companies); those that are personal-at-work-related (e.g. the CEO relationship with the Chairman, dysfunctional top team, lack of skill in specific areas); and those that are purely personal (e.g. retire in five years' time, switch to a different sector for new experience, give more time to my family). Invariably these individual objectives may not always align with those of the business and organization. In this chapter, we are concerned with how to achieve alignment in helping clients meet business priorities and with evaluation of whether these business priorities are being met.

'The Theatre of Business'

In William Shakespeare's play *As You Like It* are the famous lines:

> *'All the world's a stage, and all the men and women merely players.*
> *They have their exits and their entrances; and one man in his time*
> *plays many parts, his acts being seven ages ...'*

This chapter illustrates a model of how the 'coach', the 'client' (the person being coached) and the 'sponsor' (the person representing the organization within which the client works) work together. They individually and collectively have priorities and purposes to increase the business performance of the organization. How they know if they have met these business priorities and purposes is the key issue during and at the end of the coaching relationship.

As their lives unfold, men and women play many parts on the stage of the world. This theatrical analogy provides a metaphor for examining a client's role in their own work life. In Fig. 10.1 we depict the 'Theatre of Business' in which the sponsor, client and coach are all operating.

Prologue/director/producer

In Shakespeare's *Troilus and Cressida*, the Prologue sets the stage for the play by outlining the war between the Greeks and the Trojans, led by Menelaus and Priam. We as readers and watchers need to know something of these 'broils', otherwise the rest of the play will be meaningless. The prologue says therefore:

> *'And hither am I come*
> *A prologue arm'd ...*
> *To tell you, fair beholders, that our play*
> *Leaps o'er the vaunt and firstlings of these broils,*
> *Beginning in the middle; starting thence away*
> *To what may be digested in a play.'*

As the play unfolds, the history and setting can then be referred to at will by Shakespeare to give even richer meaning to the action. The director or producer will also give his or her interpretation of how the play should unfold to all the various actors and actresses.

In the coaching context, the 'sponsor' gives a brief which acts like the prologue, as well as the director/producer's interpretation. The coach

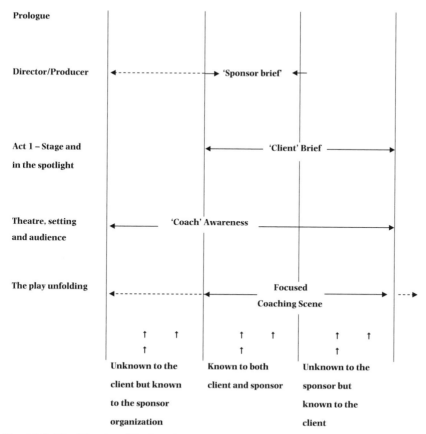

Fig. 10.1 The 'Theatre of Business'

needs to know the current state of the business, its history and relevant details. A large amount can be obtained from Annual Reports, news data, the internet and other business search engines, but it will be the anecdotal as much as the informed which will give meaning to the 'action of coaching' which ensues. Culture, personal targets for the client, strategic aims of the business, interplays with other directors and executives, key performance indicators for the business, impending business changes (organizationally and operationally), industry competition and comparative data all have a part to play – the list is long, but necessary.

Some of this sponsor briefing may be known to the coach but not to the client. For example, the sponsor may have confided in the coach that the client is potentially earmarked as CEO in five years' time, but may not have been so specific with the client when saying that 'you have strong potential to get on in this organization.'

The coach is not meant to become an overnight expert, but their understanding of the business, both through experience and briefing, will be enhanced and will bring benefit to the coach/client relationship.

Act 1 on stage/play unfolding

The client will give his own brief to the coach on what is significant in this particular 'play' and what he wishes to work on. The coach is a personal coach to the actor and will be as concerned for him in this role as for his development, which will equip him for his next role. The coach's concern will be for his effectiveness as a performer and his wellbeing as an actor on this business stage. The producer ('sponsor') will want to bring out the best in the actor in the context of how he sees the play being interpreted.

As the play unfolds, the producer may change the setting, costumes, layout or backdrops, and may cut or even embellish scenes. All these things could change the outcome intended, and at any one time many aspects of changes to be made by the sponsor will be unknown to the client. The client will be increasingly aware of his needs, wants and aspirations as an actor, which he does not as yet wish to bring to the attention of the producer but will happily work on with his coach 'offstage' in the meanwhile.

The coach will become more and more aware of the other actors and actresses through the references made by the client in his speeches, descriptions of scenes and interactions, and through direct knowledge via discussion and observation. He will be aware of the wider audience, the acoustics, the auditorium, etc.

Bertha: an illustration

Bertha is a Commercial Director in a multi-billion primarily European company in the healthcare industry. The prime sponsor in this coach/client relationship is the HR Director, who initiated a briefing session with the coach. Bertha is being groomed for the UK Managing Director role, but has some 'rough edges'. The organization is growing rapidly but at present there is only one CEO role, which is CEO of both UK and Continental Europe. Because of growth, this role should be split and the overall Chairman and board want this to happen. The present CEO has grown up with the business and been instrumental in its growth, and is reluctant to give up the role. The client does not know this, nor does the coach.

The presented issue for coaching is that the CEO (having asked the client to 'rattle cages' in his absence at the Executive Team meetings) and the HR Director are concerned that Bertha is upsetting Executive Team members and is tending to act as the Managing Director too much.

Bertha admits that she is competitive and has to win, and is OK about the prospect of becoming UK MD, but she is concerned about being 'reprimanded' for doing what she has been asked to do, i.e. 'rattle cages'. Some 360° work by the coach introduces the perspective of all the other Executive Team members into the process of Bertha's development into a potential MD role. They are concerned about Bertha's 'rattling cages' agenda, but are more aware of her need to slow down, act collaboratively, show her capability to think strategically and to give credit and recognition to other functions/departments and not just her own.

The coach works with Bertha on a major competitive tender for sales to the National Health Service, which necessitates cooperation with other departments. It allows Bertha to work with others on developing the values of the organization and seeing how they work through into operational systems and processes.

While this is going on, the coach becomes aware through the HR Director that an external search in the UK for a new UK MD is being undertaken by head hunters. The client (and the coach up until now) is unaware that she has any competition for the role of UK MD: she has been advised to the contrary by the CEO. The CEO is using the external search mechanism to 'prove' that no UK candidates are available, thus ensuring that no UK MD can be appointed. It now becomes apparent that the CEO has no intention of considering Bertha as the UK MD. The coaching now takes on a different agenda.

A series of meetings between the coach, the client, the CEO and the HR Director bring key issues onto the agenda. After some very difficult discussions with all the parties and considering resignation, Bertha is asked to meet the Chairman for a discussion about a possible UK MD role. The whole process (which has taken a year so far) has made Bertha aware that she will have greater influence by remaining as Commercial Director than by becoming UK MD. The organization is now forced to run a Europe-wide external search, run by the Chairman who now takes personal responsibility for the split in the role of European CEO.

In this case involving Bertha, despite the initial briefing, the real clarity over the business priorities emerged much later. The agenda and outcomes of coaching were being redefined constantly in the light of meetings with the HR Director, CEO and other directors. It was not an easy situation for the coach to work in. What can we learn from this about how the coach, client and sponsor can best achieve the business priorities for the client and the organization?

We will consider this in three areas: within the sponsor organization, within the coaching firm and within the coaching process.

Focusing coaching to address business priorities

1: Within the sponsor organization

Sponsor briefing

While it is often an organizational representative (CEO or HR Director) who will provide a briefing to the coach about the client and their organization, there are valuable ways of supplementing this. For example, Zurich Financial Services, as well as providing an individual who is a focal point for coaching who can provide an individual 'pen portrait' of the client and their circumstances, also provides an induction for coaches. This involves a half-day seminar where coaches are provided with the same material about Zurich's 'basics' and its organizational strategy as are employees. Matt Williams, Senior Development Consultant in the Talent Learning and Development Shared Service, says: 'If an employee needs to understand about Zurich to fulfil their role as a colleague, then all our suppliers, including coaches, should have the same experience. It sends the right signals about what kind of company we strive to be and how we want to succeed.'

The result for the coach is an awareness of what the organization is aiming to achieve and the strategic approach it will take, and thus what is expected of the client.

Briefing coaches in groups

As well as bringing coaches together to brief them on the organization's strategy, some organizations go through a briefing process with the coaches they are using. This is an opportunity to outline what is expected of coaches and an opportunity for the business to identify coaches who will help them meet their strategic needs. Unilever undertake assessment of coaching capability through a series of discussions with and presentations from external coaches. One investment bank has organized international conference calls for coaches who have previously submitted CVs in a particular format to discuss generic issues arising out of the coaching, and they are thus able to provide feedback on the agenda items contracted to be discussed. All this is done while maintaining strict individual direct confidentiality.

PepsiCo's International Director of Organization and Management Development in New York is David Oliver. He is responsible for maintaining

PepsiCo's coaching network for the international division. PepsiCo's certification programme for coaches takes place in New York and they have also held programmes in various parts of the world depending on the region of interest. The purpose of the certification programme is to create alignment on the PepsiCo international talent management approach, to educate coaches on the tools used by PepsiCo – both internal and external – and to evaluate the coaches. The evaluation gives David and his team a sense of how effective the coach will be, and what types of executives to pair them with.

2: Within the coaching firm

Where several coaches are operating within the same organization working with several different client executives simultaneously, the opportunities for meeting the business priorities are enhanced significantly.

Generic feedback

A major utilities organization operating across many sites both in the UK and America was concerned about developing its next-generation leaders. A programme was devised which included key faculty members from Duke University in the States, together with members of the organization. External coaches were engaged from our organization to assist the next-generation leaders to identify their own specific Personal Development Plans. This was approached via a three-way meeting (see below in the section entitled *Within the coaching process*) with the next-generation leaders boss.

Because several coaches were used, we were able to collate our ideas with the organization's representative. Without betraying any confidentiality, we were able to give feedback on key issues relating to the need for strategic thinking and particular aspects of commerciality. The coaches in their individual client engagements were able to understand the organizational issues from different perspectives. The organization could then act upon the generic feedback provided.

Highlighting trends

While coaches can feed back in an unattributed way, the information provided to them separately, they can also provide deep insights into what they are learning.

In one organization in the international property development and real estate industry, this meant that the company heard about the deep cultural issues which were surfacing. The executive team were encouraging and promoting teamwork and an 'anti-silo' mentality, but at the same time nothing was being done about the reward and bonus systems which remunerated individuals and promoted 'silo mentality'.

In another banking organization, the knowledge gleaned by coaches about time pressures, performance focus and short-term results, fed into the observation about the lack of career discussions held with senior members of the bank. High-potentials were being well rewarded monetarily, but there was little discussion about the 'value and worth' of the individual high-potential executive in non-monetary terms: 'Where is my career going in the Bank?'; 'What is the next sensible role for me?'. By highlighting this growing trend in demand for career discussions, the coaches were able to assist the HR function in their ongoing attempts to raise the issue with senior management. The data was now available.

3: Within the coaching process

Three-way meetings
At the start of a coaching programme, it is increasingly the case that the coach and the client are joined for a discussion by the client's boss. This ensures that the middle column in the earlier diagram (Fig. 10.1 on page 147) is absolutely clear from the outset. What the boss expects the coaching to provide for the individual and the organization becomes openly discussed. Both coach and client hear the same language, and there is a reference point for use as necessary at later stages as the agenda is worked through: 'This is what we agreed we were going to do, so have we done it yet?'

Contracting
Where a contract is established between the client, the coach and the sponsor, everyone is clear about the likely outcomes. It can include words agreed by the client and coach, which become three or four key items for the coaching agenda. Measurable outcomes are agreed which are framed in observable or behavioural terms, e.g. 'X will demonstrate strategic thinking capability in Executive Team meetings' or 'Senior staff will see Y's leadership style as more consensual and less autocratic'.

Personal Development Plans
Following attendance at a business school or leadership programme, senior managers invariably return with the germ of an agenda for their own development. External coaches are able to work with them in expressing this in the context of their business and as a personal development plan (PDP). This will have specific objectives which will be addressed through the coaching process and a PDP, at a summary level, can be shared by the

executive with the organization. This ensures an element of personal and shared accountability for the results of the coaching.

Evaluation of coaching work

Key ingredients of effective evaluation of coaching to test whether it meets business objectives include the following.

- **Initial evaluation at the end of the first meeting between coach and coaches**: a very deliberate review at the end of the first meeting enables the coachee to say that they do not want to continue if they do not think the coaching is going to be worthwhile. There should be a very clear expectation on a coach to be explicit at the end of the first meeting about their view of whether the coaching work is going to be fruitful.
- **Self validation**: the individual client will normally be the first to indicate whether value is being obtained from the coaching sessions as they progress. If they begin to cancel meetings this is often evidence that the coaching is not proving as worthwhile as it should be.
- **Written 360° feedback**: where a written 360° methodology is available to members of the organization, this can provide a valuable means of seeing whether progress is being made. The exercise can be undertaken at the start and towards the latter part of the coaching relationship to determine how much progress has been made.
- **Oral 360° feedback**: face-to-face or telephone discussions between the coach and an individual's boss, peers and direct reports can provide very powerful feedback about strengths to build on and areas for development. This can provide a powerful input to coaching and a benchmark for further feedback to identify progress. This process would be undertaken by the coach interviewing between six and eight people.
- **Views of individual clients**: the specific views of coachees at the end of each programme are a crucial ingredient. Ideally the evaluation form is worked out jointly with the relevant coaching organizations and there is ownership of both the evaluation process and taking forward the results.
- **Assessment of clients**: clients will have received appraisals, psychometric test results, organizational assessment or 360° feedback, and this can be used in the coaching process. Over the course of a year, the business cycle may encompass a further interaction of these assessments: it is then possible to make comparisons of outcomes.
- **Views at the end of the coaching**: an examination of the sponsor brief and of the expectations set at the outset can take place at the end of

the coaching period. These expectations may be seen in terms of behaviours, competences, skills, learning, relationships, style, understanding, etc., all of which can be observed.

Conclusion

A Shakespearian play had a purpose. It was written to be performed and acted and to entertain on a stage. There will have been many other purposes as it was performed, e.g. to enhance the reputation of the playwright, to make money for the theatre owner, etc.

Organizations and businesses have purposes – and not just to make profit or to meet shareholder demands. Identifying the key purposes and their priorities in relation to any executive's coaching programme will be the precursor to establishing the best means of achieving those business priorities.

Chapter 11:

Introducing Coaching Programmes into an Organization

This chapter focuses on introducing coaching programmes into an organization. It addresses a range of important considerations, in particular:

- what are the most important ingredients of success;
- characteristics of successful coaching;
- what are you looking for in a coaching organization;
- what feedback and evaluation do you particularly want to see out of coaching;
- what are the pitfalls which need to be watched;
- ensuring quality in coaching programmes;
- where do psychometrics fit in;
- where do different psychological approaches fit in;
- good practice in practical coaching arrangements;
- illustrative coaching arrangements covering a UK government department, a leading financial institution and a leading professional services organization; and
- bringing a coaching programme to effective conclusion.

It suggests that the next steps in introducing coaching programmes relate to clarity about the business context, the coaching choices and the method used to implement coaching. A self-contained coaching tool is set out in Annex 1 which can be applied by individual purchasing organizations.

Introducing coaching programmes effectively in an organization depends on the effective engagement with a number of different strands. It needs to start from a clear perception about what is success, and what is meant by 'quality' in coaching organizations with guarantees about the quality of the coaching and sound supervision. Choices about the use of psychometrics and physiologically based approaches play an important part in

Fig. 11.1 Factors involved in deciding about coaching programmes

decisions about coaching programmes and the buying of coaching. These strands are summarized in Fig.11.1.

What are the most important ingredients for success?

Those with a long experience of buying coaching see the following as the most important ingredients of success.

'A tailored programme including semi-structured 360° interviews.'
                                                              Noel Hadden

'Helping an individual understand the shadow they cast as a leader. Oral 360° feedback can show a leader what their shadow is like, how the impact is felt as against how it is intended.'   Hilary Douglas

'Clarity about why coaching is being brought in and the selection of the right coaches. Coaching without clarity can release unexpected consequences.'

Jim McCaffery

'Making sure that both for the overall coaching programme and individual interventions you know where the destination is – i.e. be clear where you want the coaching to lead.'

Rob Edwards

'Clear objectives. Doing coaching for the right reasons. Ensuring the importance of tough love. The coach and client need to be comfortable with each other. There needs to be a flexible arrangement whereby the client is able to phone up for a conversation. The coach needs to be able to adapt to the rhythm. It is important to strike the balance between the coach being a sounding-board and someone who gives input. There needs to be a degree of mutual self-awareness and diagnosis.'

Jill King

'People get too focused on models and processes when coaching is about a conversation. What is so important is a genuine relationship. Having a conversation which adds value to the individual is more important than being precious about any particular model.'

John Bailey

'Clear outcomes. Being sure what you are trying to achieve and focusing it into a particular period.'

Philippa Charles

Characteristics of successful coaching

Distilling the wisdom of organizations who are ensuring successful coaching for their staff points to a set of key principles. An organization that wants to make a success of coaching will:

- be clear about what its own objectives and values are;
- be clear what it wants its senior and middle managers to be focusing on and delivering;
- have an accurate assessment of the interrelationship between competences in the organization and desired outcomes of coaching;

- be clear what the development needs of individuals are in both the short and longer term;
- be able to differentiate between the needs of different groups in terms of their development; and
- be able to articulate a clear prospectus of the coaching needs within the organization.

It is helpful to consider the different priority groups and decide where investment is going to produce the biggest dividends. Potential groups for this purpose might be the top team, those promoted to a new grade, individuals knocking on the door of promotion, high potential staff, individuals who have behavioural needs which need to be addressed because specific behaviours are holding them back or those who need to move on either within the organization or outside but who need the stimulus to ensure they take next steps effectively.

The organization needs to be as clear as possible about the specific business benefits it is seeking in relation to each target group. There will be short-term benefits. Hilary Douglas commented that, 'Coaching seems to have made the most immediate difference when behavioural characteristics are getting in the way. If an individual never goes out of his office, changing that person's behaviour patterns and the way they interrelate with others can happen quickly and dramatically.'

In some cases the impact of the coaching will be longer-term as an individual gets much better at using their time effectively and facing up to difficult issues. To achieve successful outcomes from short-term coaching programmes it is necessary for leaders to be confident about the prospect of benefits over the long term.

What are you looking for in a coaching organization?

A key step is to reflect on the type of coaching organization you want to work with. Coaching organizations come in many different shapes and sizes. Some coaching organizations have a particular focus on business coaching whereas others come from a more psychologically based approach. Some organizations are a loose grouping of individuals whereas others have a more specific or coherent culture. Views of those with a long experience of purchasing coaching are as follows:

> 'I look for companies with a strength in depth from "pinstripes" to "white coats". There must be consistency in output. I am not looking for a common methodology but the results must be consistent. I'm looking

for stability in a coaching partner where their business is coaching. The organization must understand supervision and use it effectively. There needs to be good quality data fed back to the organization about generic themes. There needs to be a single point of contact. It is crucial that individual coaches are not incentivized to recommend themselves but will always recommend the most suitable person. It is important that a coaching organization is not linked to a particular head-hunter because impartiality is fundamental.'

Noel Hadden

'I look for coaching organizations which provide a choice of coaches with a variety of styles so that there can be a matching up of the right chemistry. Sometimes the individual might be sceptical about coaching so ensuring that the right type of coach is appointed is crucial.'

Hilary Douglas

'I look for the experience of a multi-led approach. I want an organization who can bring in different levels of experience from different environments. It is important that the coaches have clout: they need to be comfortable and confident in the board room. I need people with credibility and experience. They must always be positive and not superannuated cynics.'

Jim McCaffery

'I am looking for organizations who will work happily and enthusiastically in partnership. Organizations need to be ready to provide tailored coaching and not coaching that is just off the peg. I look for a speed of response that is quick. I look for the honesty bit in terms of feedback. I need to know when progress is being made and when is the right time to complete a coaching programme. I want the coachee to get personal treatment but there needs to be rigour about when there are diminishing returns.'

Rob Edwards

'I prefer to work with a coaching organization than a group of associates. It is important that different types of coaches can be matched with different people. It is important that the partnership works effectively with a coaching organization. When this type of body understands as well their coaches will be able to challenge individuals the more effectively.'

Jill King

'I look carefully at the reputation of the organization. What are the relationship skills of the people I meet? The organization needs to be sensitive to what will work in terms of compatibility.'

John Bailey

'I'm looking for a good range of different coaches from different perspectives. There must be a willingness to understand our business. The coaches need to understand our culture and operating style. There needs to be a flexible approach to how the coaching is structured. I need to have confidence that the coaches are professionally trained and experienced. The coaches need to include people with experience of different cultures.'

Philippa Charles

Another buyer of coaching emphasized that 'I look for a coaching organization with a strong sense of ethics, a wealth of coaching experience who wants to work in partnership with us and understands our issues and how coaching fits into our leadership agenda.'

When choosing a coaching organization the buyer of coaching needs to be clear what sort of coaches they want and what sort of organization is best likely to provide the type of coaches they want.

In choosing a coaching organization some of the key elements are:

- the quality of individual coaches and the mix of experience of the coaching team;
- the extent to which they draw on leadership and coaching experience in a wide range of different contexts;
- the extent to which the organization is pushing the boundaries of thought leadership (are the coaches leading the thinking in key areas?);
- the incentive structure within the coaching organization so it is clear that the right coach will be selected, with the coaching programme going on for no longer than is necessary;
- the continuous professional development arrangements for the coaches and professional supervision;
- the quality control arrangements for the coaching;
- the evaluation arrangements for the outcome of the coaching;
- the quality of the account management processes with clarity of responsibility on a single account manager;
- the capacity of the coaching organization to understand your needs;
- the speed and receptiveness of the coaching organization in responding to your needs;
- the quality of generic feedback which the coaching organization will give you arising from themes they identify within their coaching work;

- the quality of the early warning that you are given if there are problems; and
- the way the organization shares its wider professional understanding about developments in learning and leadership with your organization.

One theme to note from all the above is that not only does the organization choose a coaching provider, the individual also chooses the coach. Sometimes the individual might be sceptical about coaching. The individual will certainly not accept coaching if they can't 'accept' the coach. Individuals should and must have the right to turn down one coach in favour of another. The 'chemistry' between coach and client is crucial. Throughout all these questions a key theme is assurance about quality of both the coach, the coaching and the coaching provider.

What feedback and evaluation do you particularly want to see out of coaching?

One of the indents above was the quality of generic feedback which the coaching organization will give arising out of themes they identify within their coaching work. The views of our experts who buy coaching on feedback and evaluation are as follows:

'I want clear feedback from individuals and their line managers. It is crucial that individuals are demonstrating changes in performance as a result of the coaching.'

Noel Hadden

'The coachee must be able to demonstrate what they have achieved plus clear independent verification. Effective valuation is very important.'

Hilary Douglas

'I want people to own their own coaching programmes. It is helpful to have some organizational feedback at a generic level but that is not the principal benefit. Coaching is a relationship intervention building a commitment into individuals to focus their performance.'

Jim McCaffery

'Coaching needs predicted steps with clarity about whether the purposes have happened.'

Rob Edwards

'I don't expect to get feedback on individuals. I do expect to know what overall objectives are being worked on at individual level. There should be a two-way flow with the coaching organization about themes that are emerging.'

Jill King

'I want individual feedback from the client about the effectiveness of the coach. I want the sponsor's feedback about how the individual has developed. I don't want the arrangements to be bogged down with bits of paper. The measure has to be how has somebody benefited as an individual.'

John Bailey

'I want a clear set of goals and outcomes for coaching programmes. I don't expect to know the details of what happens in coaching meetings. I expect the client to brief HR about progress with the coaching.'

Philippa Charles

The themes cover a range of different types of feedback. Has the coaching helped somebody achieve their goals? Has there been a clear impact from the coaching a year on? It isn't just about the individual being happy with the immediate experience but also with its long term impact: what has it done to their long term energy levels within the organization?

At the heart of these comments is the balance between the confidentiality of individual coaching meetings and the importance of generic feedback. All are concerned about the importance of being clear on the effectiveness of individual coaching programmes. They want hard data on the progress of coaching and they see this particularly coming from the line manager and the individual.

What are the pitfalls which particularly need to be watched?

Introducing coaching effectively does require vigilance in a number of key areas. Some of the pitfalls identified by these buyers of coaching are:

'You have to watch dependency: the coachee must not become dependent on the coach. You need to be clear about the right time for the coaching relationship to end. It is very easy to get coaches in the system and lose track and not have clarity about the right time of the completion of the coaching programme. It is important that the matching process be-

tween coach and coachee is right. Semi-structured 360° interviews are an essential part of the process: if an individual is reluctant to do 360° feedback then there is a potential problem which needs addressing.'

Noel Hadden

'The coaching relationship can get too comfortable and roll on. An individual coachee may be enjoying have the conversations but with diminishing returns because the focus on business needs has become less strong. It is crucial to have review points when there is clarity about next steps for the coaching. The biggest risk is not defining desired outcomes at the start. Just saying, "There will be benefit from having a coach" is an abrogation of responsibility. It needs to be more sharply focused.'

Hilary Douglas

'You cannot dump an individual on a coach. You have to accept your responsibilities as a manager to that individual. Sometimes coaching is used as a conscience event when there needs to be a more thought through strategy for turning things round with one individual. It is important to ensure that coaching is followed up with different focused types of intervention.'

Jim McCaffery

'It is crucial to get the balance right between meeting individual needs and the organization's needs. Having a coach must not become a mark of status or a glorified designer label.'

Rob Edwards

'There are two main pitfalls. Firstly a lack of clear objectives at an early stage. Secondly the danger that somebody thinks it is a badge of honour to have a coach. There is a danger that coaching could go to people who do not need it because of this badge of honour effect.'

Jill King

'Coaching must be seen as a response to business issues, not just "we need a coaching culture and therefore we are going to give everyone a coach". We need to avoid the blanket approach where we wallpaper coaches across a large population. It's important to create intelligent customers and help them with making the right buying decision. A key feature of a coaching culture is people seeking out coaching from their colleagues and proactively seeking opportunities to coach others.'

John Bailey

'You need an agreed set of rules of engagement and clear outcomes. There needs to be a management of expectations for all concerned. There must be some measures of success. Confidentiality is crucial.'

Philippa Charles

Some themes include the readiness of an individual to be coached and to be focused in taking it forward. It must be clear that the coach, coachee and organization are working in tune with each other. If the line manager is not engaged there can be severe limitations on the effect of the coaching.

The key strands coming out of these comments are the importance of watching out for the pitfalls of:

- unconscious collusion between coach and client to avoid the difficult issues and be too cosy;
- the problems that can occur if clear objectives are not set;
- the importance of matching coach and client;
- the importance of the willingness of an individual to go through a coaching programme;
- getting the balance right between individual and organizational needs; and
- a clear set of rules of engagement and clear outcomes.

Avoiding these pitfalls is best ensured through the quality of engagement between the sponsoring organization and the coaching organization. The personal and account management links need to be strong, flexible and able to address tough issues quickly.

Ensuring quality in coaching programmes

Any coaching organization should have a robust policy on quality and evaluation. In the organization of which we are part our focus on quality includes:

- a rigorous assessment process when recruiting new members;
- 'buddying' arrangements whereby coaches are paired in order to exchange techniques and coaching approaches;
- a strong focus on continuous learning and improvement through training days, continuous professional qualifications and learning events with external speakers which ensure the coaches share experiences and keep up-to-date with new ideas and publications;
- in-house induction training for all new recruits augmented by externally accredited courses;

- regular supervision by an experienced and qualified supervisor;
- coaches meeting in groups regularly to review case studies and learn from each other's experiences; and
- the use of client satisfaction surveys carried out by an independent person covering both client organizations and individuals.

Any buying organization should satisfy itself about the quality control arrangements for any coaching organization they are seeking to use for coaching. Key questions could be:

- What level of senior leadership experience have your coaches had?
- What is their mix of current coaching practice?
- What are the level of coaching qualifications and the arrangements for continuous professional development?
- How do the coaches keep themselves refreshed?
- How available are the coaches for urgent conversations on the telephone?
- What are the individual incentives on coaches in terms of how they match coach and coaches?
- How does the coaching organization measure success?

It is worth asking a coaching organization what they regard as the key executive coaching competencies and how they develop and assess those competencies.

To be effective a coach must keep fresh. The good coach will bring a wealth of experience but needs to keep up-to-date within the coaching profession and in their understanding of leadership issues. Professional updating is just as important for coaches as any other profession.

Where do psychometrics fit in?

Psychometric assessments have been increasingly used as a means of building awareness about an individual's preferred approaches. Many leading development programmes will include the use of psychometrics which can provide valuable input into coaching. Individual coaches may favour the use of particular psychometric tools.

The benefits of psychometric tools are:

- they help build self-awareness;
- they can highlight preferences and motivations which may not be obvious;

- clarity about strengths enables an individual to use their strengths more effectively;
- they identify least preferred style of approaches which may need developing if the individual is to widen their repertoire of ways of responding to diverse situations;
- they can be particularly useful in a team to build awareness of the strengths and weaknesses and preferred approaches of different members of a team;
- they enable a coach to understand an individual's preferred approaches so enabling them to work with the coachees the more effectively;
- they can provide clarity and a sharper perspective on information from other sources (such as 360° feedback); and
- they open up issues for conversation about behaviours and preferences which an individual might otherwise be less willing to engage in.

The pitfalls to watch for include:

- they should not be used judgementally to reach rigid stereotype conclusions;
- if not used intelligently they can be a label or a box. A rigid definition of someone's style can be one-dimensional and it can become a self-fulfilling prophesy if someone relies on one style too much and can be an excuse for someone to perpetuate non-productive behaviour;
- the results from psychometrics should only be a starting point for discussion and are not an end in themselves;
- the coach needs to have been trained in how to provide feedback from psychometric assessments. If the coach is assessing an individual using a particular psychometric tool they need to be trained in the application of the tool. For most coaching conversations it will be training in interpreting psychometric data rather than applying the psychometric tool that is important;
- some clients may be fearful about psychometric tools and avoid them and their results at all costs (which is useful feedback in itself!); and
- there can be an over-reliance on one psychometric tool. Where two or three tools are used, the results can provide data covering a range of different perspectives. The same themes emerging from a number of instruments is hard to refute.

An important question to ask a coaching organization or coach is where do psychometric assessments fit into their coaching approach. Beware of either too heavy a reliance on psychometrics or an ignorance about their use and value. Some of the most used psychometric tools are those summarised below:

Myers-Briggs (MBTI)

This is the world's most used psychometric tool which has 50 years of research built round it. It is based on the theory of psychological type developed by Carl Jung. It is easily accessible and individuals normally recognise themselves. A recent UK study concluded that about three-quarters of people agreed with all four letters of their reported MBTI type. The tool identifies preferences and attitudes which contribute to an individual's personality.

The parameters within MBTI are:

Extroversion (E)	**Introversion (I)**	how you are energized
Sensing (S)	**Intuition (N)**	how you take in information
Thinking (T)	**Feeling (F)**	how you make decisions
Judging (J)	**Perceiving (P)**	the lifestyle you prefer.

MBTI can be particularly helpful when a team wants to understand why they make different contributions as board members. An understanding of their MBTI assessment can help an individual to decide what strengths they want to build on and what areas that are not their natural preferences they want to develop. It is the conscious development of learned behaviour in non-preference areas that often distinguishes the most successful of leaders.

The main practical uses of MBTI are:

- working out how to engage with a person of a different type;
- understanding how to accommodate the 'absence' of certain innate preferences in a board team; and
- understanding the difference between innate and learned behaviour.

NEO PI-R

Unlike MBTI, the NEO PI-R is not based on a model of theory, but uses factor analysis, a technique for analysing the underlying dimensions of many individual items. It was developed from the work of psychologist Gordon Allport drawing from an analysis of 4500 words that can be used to describe personality. Costa & McCrae used further analysis to establish 5 fundamental categories. These are often referred to as the 'Big Five' and are different to many instruments in that the scales are normally distributed spectrums rather than two different letters/types.

The five factors overlap quite a lot with the dimensions of MBTI.

1   Neuroticism or Experience of Negative Emotion – how far one is prone to experience or understand negative emotion.
2   Extraversion – how far one draws energy from others and dominates groups.
3   Openness – interest in new or unusual things.
4   Agreeableness – the value one places on relationships with others (strongly related to the MBTI T-F scale).
5   Conscientiousness – interest in leading a structured and organized life.

The various facets of NEO can be analysed in different combinations to understand various characteristics of individuals and teams.

FIRO-B

This is a personality instrument that measures how an individual typically behaves with other people and how you prefer them to act towards you. It can help an individual understand better how they relate to other people and how conflict can develop between people even though they are trying to work constructively together.

FIRO-B results can be used to show patterns of interpersonal behaviour and expectations and enable an individual to reflect on how satisfied or dissatisfied they are with those patterns.

Areas of interpersonal needs identified by FIRO-B are:

- inclusion: how much you generally include others in your life and how much attention and recognition you want from others;
- control: how much influence and responsibility you want and how much you want others to lead and influence you; and
- affection: how close and warm you are with others and how close and warm you want others to be with you.

The results cover both expressed and wanted needs. For example expressed control is about how often you act in ways that help you direct or influence situations while wanted control is about how much leadership or influence you want others to assume. FIRO-B provides a snapshot about interpersonal needs which enables someone to be more aware of their natural tendencies and thereby chose more deliberately whether a particular behaviour is, or is not, appropriate at a specific time. We have seen these FIRO-B assessments to be particularly effective when a board is looking at their respective needs in terms of how they best work together. A key practical use is aiding the understanding of the dynamics of board member relationships.

Goleman's emotional intelligence measures

Daniel has done a lot of work looking at the difference between average and outstanding performers and saw as crucial a good level of emotional intelligence. At its heart emotional intelligence is self-awareness: a sense of self-worth and self-confidence and an acknowledgement of how one's own emotions affect performance.

Emotional intelligence links together self-awareness, social awareness, self-management and relationship management. Self-awareness together with social awareness (having empathy with others either as individuals or as a group and seeing and meeting other's needs) enables individuals to better manage two different areas: the first is managing themselves (emotional self-control, flexibility in handling change and maintaining integrity, together with initiative, optimism and an achievement orientation) and the second is managing relationships (developing others, inspiring leadership, managing change, influencing with impact, resolving conflict and working collaboratively). A key practical use is determining how leadership styles and emotional intelligence are linked and how flexible a leader can be in whichever style they adopt.

Thomas Kilman conflict resolution tool

This looks at how an individual handles conflict using the 5 strands of:

- avoidance;
- accommodation;
- competition;
- compromise; and
- collaboration.

It helps identify how much an individual naturally needs to respond to others' interests and how much value they place on relationships. This tool has been particularly helpful in enabling individuals to understand difficult relationships. Sometimes individuals can seem to perennially enjoy being in conflict. The use of this tool highlights that tendency and enables a constructive discussion about using different approaches to resolve problems. Both of us have used this tool to powerful effect in enabling people to focus constructively on their next steps in moving relationships on to a more productive level.

Belbin's team roles

This highlights the kind of role an individual prefers to adopt in team situations. The use of this approach has enabled members of a team to understand their different contributions more effectively. Knowing your own primary contribution and the presence or absence of other key contributions can be very revealing for a team in thinking how best it can work. A key practical use is providing a trigger for thinking about how a board team functions and interacts and what can be done to make it more effective as a team.

Where do different psychological approaches fit in?

The most discussed psychologically derived approaches are NLP (Neuro-Linguistic Programming) CBT (Cognitive Behaviour Therapy) TA (Transactional Analysis) and solution-based approaches. These all provide valuable insights. The good coach will understand these approaches and draw from them in their coaching practice. But over-reliance on one approach can produce a one-dimensional style of coaching.

The kernel of these approaches are as follows:

NLP

This approach has been particularly useful in enabling people to think about their sense of identify and purpose. It enables individuals to think much more positively about their current situation and view any sense of failure as a positive rather than negative step.

CBT

The simple truth that changing attitudes can influence behaviour is at the heart of much good coaching work. The coaches may or may not define it as CBT but helping an individual to think through how their thought processes are the key determinates of their action and behaviour can enable somebody to be less captive to their own preconceptions.

Transactional analysis

For many leaders under stress there is the danger of a habitual reaction which comes from ingrained behaviour. The reaction under pressure to give a childlike response can hold an individual back. Enabling themselves to look above that danger can help an individual move on to a new set of learnt conditioned responses.

Solution-based approaches

The continued focus on the positive in the solution based approach has worked well with many clients. Helping an individual put a problem into a wider perspective and enabling them to move on in a new way can be powerful.

Good practice in practical coaching arrangements

To be effective one-to-one coaching needs to be a conversation in a private space with no interruptions. Ideally it is away from the individual's work context so that there is a detachment. It can work well at the workplace provided there are no distractions: i.e. a private room with no interruptions

The ideal coaching discussions are between 1½ and 2 hours long with a regular sequence of meetings. If an individual is going through major difficulties there might be a need for a rapid sequence of coaching discussions. More normally the discussions would take place on about a monthly to six weekly basis.

An initial coaching programme covering a year allows for development in a variety of areas although some organizations focus on 6 months in the first instance. There always needs to be clarity about the outcomes to be sought in the coaching programme and how progress is going to be measured.

Meeting on the basis of once a month to 6 weeks keeps within reasonable bounds the time commitment for the individual and leaves plenty of time between meetings for taking forward the learning from the coaching conversations. There would normally be a commitment at the end of each coaching session about next steps with the coach holding the client to account at the start of the subsequent meeting about what had worked and what had not worked. A sequence of 6 or 12 coaching sessions allows areas where progress is needed to be fully explored with the testing of progress. This length of time also allows scope for oral 360° feedback as part of the coaching programme.

Sometimes coaching addresses focused needs where three sessions will provide the right scope. For example if somebody is working on personal impact leading up to a major interview, three sessions will provide the opportunity to look at the specific needs, develop a strategy, experiment with a strategy and embed what has worked well.

The ideal coaching programme will involve more than just face-to face discussions. 360° oral feedback is a supplement which organizations are increasingly regarding as essential. There is plenty of scope for innovation. For example a coach might spend a day with a coachee observing them in meetings which they chair or are a member of, talking to immediate colleagues and then feeding back in a coaching session towards the end of the day. In this way the coach builds a picture of the impact an individual is having in the workplace.

We now turn to three examples of coaching arrangements which are working well covering:

- a UK government department;
- a leading financial institution; and
- a leading professional services organization.

Illustrative coaching arrangements: a government department

This government department has put a particular emphasis on executive coaching as part of its leadership development. It has a contract with four different providers of executive coaching who bring a variety of approaches. In their literature they describe coaching in the following way,

> 'Many senior executives choose to address their personal development, or supplement other development action, through one-to-one coaching. Coaching is for people who have the ambition to be the very best leaders they can, and who know that this can only be done through critical honesty and self-awareness. Coaching provides a focus on helping an individual to address the issues that they find the most demanding: the private space of coaching enables these issues to be tackled in a way which is highly effective and personal. Coaches are critical friends – maintaining a high level of challenge alongside watertight confidentiality, a strong, supportive approach and a true professional interest in enabling you to achieve to achieve your full potential.'

They describe the type of situations where coaching could be particularly useful as including:

- increasing your confidence in how you present ideas;
- honing your personal impact;
- analysing and optimizing your performance in meetings and presentations;
- working through periods of business change;
- being successful in a new demanding role or promotion;
- increasing self-awareness;
- clarifying vision and working through priorities; and
- dealing effectively with difficult situations.

The department sought feedback from the initial group of individuals who had been through coaching. Some of the key conclusions from the feedback analysis were as follows:

- in 90% of cases both the coachee and coach said that development objectives had been met both at the end of the intervention and 6 months later;
- in 90% of cases the coachee said that coaching has made them more self-aware and able to assess their own performance more effectively;
- in fewer than 20% of cases the coachee said that they are concerned that their performance might slip now that coaching has come to an end;
- in 100% of cases the coachee says that they could trust their coach and were comfortable talking honestly and openly with them; and
- in 80% of cases the coachee says their coaching was challenging and didn't let them off the hook on difficult issues.

Some of the comments reported to their Personnel Department about the coaching were:

- 'Coaching has been helpful in (i) rehearsing options for handling some critical problems and identifying alternative approaches which I would not have done alone (ii) offering working styles which can be used in different environments (iii) improving self-awareness of personal strengths and areas for development';
- 'Quite a lot of what I've learnt or have greater awareness of will take time to embed. I expect what I've learnt to make me a better leader and to do my job better – I'm not there yet, but expect to be in a few months' time.'

- 'Better time management, better prioritization and delegation, more comfortable in challenging in senior meetings.'
- 'The coaching was successful, not because I learnt (actually re-learnt) some techniques that are helpful for those formal occasions, but because we undertook a much broader-based analysis of where I am strong and where I have weaknesses. The coach brought out those strengths and instilled in me the confidence to rest heavily upon them and then made them the centre of my efforts to improve. This is a significant change of focus from the approach of so much of previous performance "development needs". The coach's intervention has had the effect of improving my performance across the board by exploiting my newly analysed strengths.'
- 'I was able to reappraise my thoughts and views on my own performance and capability, which had been limiting me.'
- 'The coach has genuinely coached, rather than taught or directed, and has shown quick insights into the areas we have discussed. I have found one simple thing most valuable – and I hadn't thought of it before – which is that one should concentrate on strengths, rather than focus on weaknesses and try and fix them. The coach has taken me through a sharp confidence building curve. I have been surprised how quick it was.'

Judith has coordinating responsibility for the coaching programme. For her the coaching programme is about enabling people to get better at doing their jobs. It has taken people to places where they can appraise themselves and appraise the business more effectively. It is building more resilience in a time of constant change and enabling people to recognize their strengths and weaknesses and then build on their strengths.

She comments: 'Senior leaders can sometimes get to a plateau in their work, and coaching can have a particular effect in saying "Where do I go now – what can I work on next? How do I get to the next level in my own performance?"'

In choosing coaching organizations to work with she was looking for people who were straightforward to work with on a day-to-day basis. She was looking for real professionalism. She chooses to work with organizations that are specialist coaching organizations or have a specialist coaching arm. An up-to-date knowledge of coaching is important and organizations must be savvy about the business world in which coachees are operating.

Judith looks for coaches who have a strong ability to question and draw things out. For her they must carry weight and reputation. Coaches must have insight and see what a person is about. She looks for coaches who can bring out next steps by their questions and not by telling people. Judith wants to see people saying, 'I never knew coaching could be so helpful. I feel confident that I can do my job better now.' She wants people to come out of coaching feeling upbeat about what they can do next.

After positive results from the initial group of people who had been through a coaching process the department extended the coaching work and integrated it within the overall plan for leadership development. In this second phase Directors and Deputy Directors have had three 2 hour coaching discussions which have started from written 360° feedback reports and a discussion between the coach and the individual's line manager. These two sets of data have provided a valuable starting point for the coaching.

The focus of the coaching discussions has been the preparation of a personal development plan focusing on key priorities over the next few months. The broad structure of the discussions has been:

- First coaching discussion: reflection on the lessons from the feedback and first thoughts on next steps;
- Second coaching discussion: the content of the personal development plan (PDP); and
- Third coaching discussion: taking forward elements within the PDP ensuring they are embedded.

Between the second and third discussion each individual was encouraged to have a discussion with their line manager so there is agreement about next steps and a shared perspective about desired outcomes.

Robin was one of the senior managers who has had 3 coaching discussions. His comments were:

> 'The coaching has helped me crystallize things. It has helped give discipline to my thinking and enabled me to put things into context. Turning the raw material of the 360° feedback and line manager feedback into key development areas of actions has been important. It has been very valuable to do this in the environment which has provided an opportunity to talk things through openly and clearly. It has been a clear and positive coaching prompt to action. Taking time and energy on personal development has enabled me to become bolder and focus more on communication.'

An important part of the process has been the feeding back of generic themes arising out of the coaching work to the department. Absolute confidentiality in respect of each coaching discussion has been important, but the department's senior management was conscious that carefully considered feedback from the coaching organizations would provide helpful insights into the pressure points and the appetite for development.

Illustrative coaching arrangements: a leading financial institution

Numerous financial institutions see coaching as an important development tool. This section illustrates how one such organization uses one-to-one coaching extensively as part of its focus on learning and development drawing on coaches from a number of different organizations.

They are very clear in setting out their views on coaching. They describe coaching as a 'form of on the job development to generate opportunities for learning under facilitated support and feedback. Coaching facilitates a learning process based on the appreciation of past lessons and the anticipation of future opportunities'.

They use coaching for two main reasons.

- Employees are expected to develop a wide range of technical ('expert'), problem-solving and people-handling talents as they progress in their career. Performance issues may occur when skills are incorrectly matched to the situation and in this case coaching may help to improve an individual's performance.
- Alternatively, coaching is often used to help an already high-performer with a transition into a new role or deal with new challenges.

Some examples of this are below.

- The right skills are new to the individual and/or have been practised too little.
- The individual wants to apply the skills but something gets in the way of them doing so.
- Skills are not applied at all – they stay in permanent reserve, get rusty or forgotten.
- The right skills are used in one situation but are not transferred to other situations.
- The wrong skills are applied – the individual selects the wrong skills from their skills base.
- Skills are overused or the range of skills is unbalanced.
- The right skills are applied but at the wrong time.

The organization is clear that the coaching must be grounded in the individual's current work situation and experience. They describe it as having three purposes:

- to improve the individual's awareness of his or her own behaviour (actions, thoughts and feelings);
- to allow what is being learned in the sessions to be related to real life and to provide opportunity for experimentation in new behaviour; and
- to monitor progress and allow the individual to register his or her own success.

Their guidance makes clear that the individual may be asked to monitor and keep a record of their own behaviours and their effects (as they relate to the main focus of coaching). Specific tasks can be set between sessions to test new approaches. A review of these experiments can become the central theme for the next stage.

The organization places a strong focus on confidentiality. They want the individual to feel free to explore their behaviour, motivation, thoughts and feelings within a coaching relationship that is based on trust and respect. The coach is required to keep secrets and not disclose any information of a confidential nature and is bound by the confidentiality agreement in the contract for the work. The 'sponsor' or boss is encouraged to agree the objectives for the coaching. But the areas that are 'closed' to the sponsor are the detailed content of the coaching sessions and any feedback from the coach without the explicit permission from the individual. It encourages three-way meetings between the individual, the coach and the sponsor at an early stage in the coaching so that there is a shared broad perspective on the situation and an alignment of objectives.

They see as good practice in coaching sessions:

- the individual and coach review the issue (in detail), how it influences the individual, how it affects others and patterns of behaviour, e.g. particular people or situations that influence the behaviour;
- the motivation for the behaviour is examined, both in present circumstances and in the past;
- during each session the individual is encouraged to challenge their existing way of thinking and to explore less familiar ways of learning. This is likely to be uncomfortable and tiring as it is unfamiliar territory but is the substance from which significant change emerges;
- at the end of a session the individual may be reminded of what has been achieved so far and the task to be carried out next. As coaching is an

open-ended process the task may include time for digesting, reflecting and making sense of a coaching session; and

- coaching is a cumulative process and the beginning of each new session may iterate what has gone before allowing time for review.

In a very fast moving environment, coaching has the advantage of being able to be done at a time suitable for individuals. It has proved to be a significantly attractive development opportunity with major strides being made by those receiving coaching.

Illustrative coaching arrangements: a leading professional services organization

This leading professional services organization has a strong belief in the value of both internal and external coaching. In their literature they describe coaching as '[A] direct activity which helps people to clarify their goals, develop a plan of action and improve their performance. Typical personal objectives may involve role transition, effective leadership, client relationships and business development. The value of coaching is that it is a way of learning that is highly flexible and individualized.'

They say that, 'To develop our leadership we need to provide a guided experience, help people to learn from their experiences, challenge them and provide time for reflection.' The guidance is very clear that the success of any coaching initiative will be an achievement of specific goals.

The organization has experienced and able coaches on their own staff who have been well trained. But they are clear there are situations where an external coach should be used. They state in their guidance:

'The advantage of an external coach is that they can bring an unbiased and fresh view of problems. They will also have views, knowledge and skills gained from working in other organizations. One of the main values of a coach is to have someone who holds an objective perspective and who has no baggage or investment in the outcome. It can be difficult for an internal coach to achieve this or be perceived in an impartial way. The old adage that it is "lonely at the top" is also true. The higher your position in an organization the less likely you are to receive honest and constructive feedback. A possibility of partner performance indicators is accompanied by higher levels of scrutiny. An experienced coach can fill the gap by providing frank, objective support and feedback.'

Nick is both an internal coach and coordinates work with external coaching organizations. He puts a strong emphasis on the working relationship with a coaching provider who must have a clear understanding of the organization's business. He sees his job as ensuring a strong check on the credentials of the coaches and ensuring he gets good feedback from the clients. He puts a strong emphasis on clear objectives and accountability. In identifying the potential value of coaching their internal literature is clear that a number of senior partners and business services directors have received and benefited from coaching from external coaches.

Bringing a coaching programme to an effective conclusion

Coaching programmes should go on for no longer than is necessary. There should be enough time to enable progress to be made. Effective coaching relationships can go on for much longer than a year provided there is continued refreshment as to the purposes and there are regular changes of gear to take account of new situations. Some of the most successful leaders have had coaches over a long period. The mutual understanding has been of crucial benefit, but it has only worked because of a constant re-evaluation of the coaching work.

Coaching Programmes sometimes reach a natural point where the job has been done. Paul had recently been appointed to a Regional Director post. He felt apprehensive about his new responsibilities. Although confident and assertive in his previous post, there was an insecurity about whether he had adequate technical skills and how he would influence on a broader platform. After six sessions spread over about 10 months he said that he was now confident in his Regional Director role. He had built a strong team, he had been decisive in a number of difficult situations, he had introduced new procurement arrangements and he had got key partners on board with a new direction of travel. He described the value of the coaching in the following way:

> *'The persistent working through and questioning on key issues made me think through the issues and options very thoroughly. The coach helped me create anchor points on the way where I could stop and review progress. The result was that I prepared effectively, thought through next steps and was able to make the progress which had sometimes seemed beyond my reach. The coach helped me be very clear what my strengths are: I felt reassured with my energies recharged and able to make the progress I needed. I am now passionate about where I am in the job. I need to build on that foundation.'*

Paul and the coach agreed now was the moment to stop this phase of the formal coaching relationship but they agreed to meet informally for dinner a few months later to keep in touch. This illustration demonstrates the importance of a careful stock-take at the end of a coaching programme so that there is a consolidation of learning, no sense of dependency on the coach and a strong sense of moving on.

Next steps in introducing coaching programmes

The main steps relate to context, coaching choices and coaching implementation as follows:

- getting the **context** right is about being clear on the outcomes the organization needs to deliver, what it needs of its people, how it wants those people to grow and what are the most important external factors that could affect both the business and the development and behaviours of the people within the business;
- **coaching choices** leads into the place of coaching, the outcomes that it is meant to achieve, the type of coaching organization to be used and how the value of coaching can be built up within the organization; and
- **coaching implementation** is about the practical arrangements covering how coaching is positioned in relation to other forms of learning and development, the precision of objectives for coaching, the role of the line manager and the nature of feedback and evaluation.

Within these three broad themes are a set of key questions. These are shown in Annex 1 which is a self-contained tool which can be applied by individual purchasing organizations.

Conclusion

Introducing coaching effectively needs careful planning involving both clarity and flexibility. There needs to be transparency about the outcomes sought in coaching and the business case for it. There also needs to be a flexibility in the way the coaching time is used so that it is adapted to the needs of individuals. There need to be quality controls that are clear without being bureaucratic. The arrangements need to encourage energy and innovation and not stifle the creativity which can come so poignantly out of good quality coaching where there is creative engagement between coach, client and the sponsoring organization.

Chapter 12:

Running Coaching in Your Organization

This chapter focuses on a leader introducing coaching in their part of the organization. It suggests key steps are:
- being clear on the organizational and personal needs;
- setting an example, being the role model for coaching;
- the role of the line manager;
- ensuring successful outcomes;
- piloting;
- taking forward a coaching culture; and
- persuading sceptics about coaching, and evaluation: has the coaching been supportive, challenging and stretching?

A central theme is the importance of arrangements that are rooted in business needs, adaptable to changing circumstances with effective communications ensuring good quality coaching and measurable results.

If you are considering introducing or growing coaching in your organization you need to be personally engaged in working through the options. The best guarantee of success is your being engaged with the aspects illustrated in Fig.12.1).

Being clear on needs

A key starting point is being clear about the organizational needs and the personal needs of key individuals. Effective coaching must start from clarity about both types of needs. If the starting point is just organizational needs with no regard to the starting position of individuals the coaching is unlikely to be successful. If it is just about individual needs it can sometimes

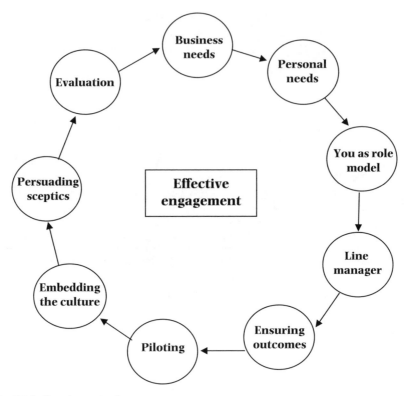

Fig. 12.1 Key elements of success

unleash energy that is not targeted on business objectives. It is important to be clear about which needs are short-term and which are long-term. Defining needs should start from as clear an understanding as possible about where an organization is going and the external business context it is facing. That provides a framework for looking at where addressing personal needs for developing confidence and competence fit in.

For a leader looking at their part of the organization key steps are:

- What is my part of the organization expected to deliver?
- Do we have the skills and competencies to be able to achieve those results?
- What are the key strengths we want to build on?
- What are the limitations of the team?
- How best can those limitations be addressed: is it through specific skills training, courses, team coaching or individual coaching?

Team coaching might be about building a corporate agenda, encouraging a unified set of values, developing a shared perspective on key issues, ensuring much stronger personal relationships, or building a shared courage to take forward difficult tasks.

When you are introducing one-to-one coaching key questions are:

- Could helping people think strategically through the use of one-to-one coaching have a worthwhile effect on the overall business?
- Are there a set of common issues that need to be tackled, e.g. partnership building?
- Are the needs specific to individuals?
- How much would it be valuable for key individuals to have a sounding-board?
- Is changing gear something that needs to be tackled if your part of the organization is going to be fully successful?
- How quickly do you want to see results?
- How much personal time are you willing to invest in ensuring coaching programmes are a success?
- How would raised self-awareness through coaching benefit the business?

One-to-one coaching is not to be pursued lightly because of the time invested in it, hence the need sometimes to differentiate between a programme for some people over a year and maybe for others a focused programme of, say, three sessions on specific issues. Whatever the length of the programme, defining the areas to be worked on at the start and the type of outcomes sought is important.

Having defined the types of outcome and the areas to be worked on, it may well be that coaching is not the right solution. There are many other interventions available in pursuing a leadership development agenda from work-shadowing, new role experience, secondment opportunities and training courses through to further education, business school programmes, focused self-development and skills acquisition.

Setting an example: being the role model for coaching

Although your primary concern might be the need for the organization to see particular individuals growing in their effectiveness, a key starting point is you as a leader. The benefits for you of being the recipient of coaching are:

- addressing specific issues which you personally need to work on to increase your effectiveness as the leader;
- being a role model so that others will be more willing to take forward coaching if you are setting an example;
- building a personal awareness about the benefits of coaching in particular circumstances and the pitfalls;
- understanding the best way of meshing coaching within wider time commitments;
- experiencing coaching will help you develop your own coaching skills in leading your own part of the organizations; and
- by using oral 360° feedback you will be inviting people to contribute to your own personal development which is likely to have a ripple effect through the organization; and
- receiving coaching will help you develop your own coaching skills in leading your own part of the organization.

Setting an example also allows you to test out the effectiveness of a particular coach or coaching organization. Names of coaches might come from the personal recommendation of colleagues, coaching organizations which are part of a framework agreement that your organization has with a limited number of suppliers or a recommendation from an organization operating in a similar type of world. It is well worth being very selective in your choice of coach and clear about the type of business experience and personal qualities you are looking for.

It is always worth ensuring there is a chemistry meeting (i.e. an initial meeting to assess whether coach and client are going to be able to work effectively together). This could either be meeting a couple of coaches and deciding which one you are going to work with best or making a provisional decision to work with a particular coach and then having a full 2-hour coaching session before making a final decision.

These two approaches are very different and both have their advantages. Key questions to ask yourself before a chemistry meeting are:

- What do I want out of the coaching?
- What is important to me in terms of effective chemistry?
- How do I want to feel at the end of the chemistry meeting in terms of being supported or challenged?
- How important is it to me that the coach has a similar or different perspective?
- How will I judge success at the end of the chemistry meeting?

A good chemistry meeting should involve a warmth of personal exchange, the initial steps of two people getting to know each other, some coaching work on specific issues and some practical activity to then be taken forward.

Key questions to ask yourself at the end of the chemistry meeting are:

- How well has the coach understood the context in which I work?
- Did I sense that they were beginning to understand me as a person?
- How good a listener were they?
- Did their questions begin to go to the heart of the matter?
- How would I feel if the coach began to challenge and stretch me?
- Did the coach begin to help me think in a new way?
- Were there some clear points for action at the end of the session?
- How well did we engage, both at an intellectual and emotional level?
- Did I like the coach enough to spend a significant amount of time in their presence?

Once you have selected who to work with as a coach key questions are:

- Where are you going to meet (it must be a confidential private space, preferably outside your immediate workplace)?
- At what time of day are you going to meet (most coaches will want to be flexible about the timing)?
- What is the right frequency (is it monthly initially and then less frequently in a second phase)?
- How structured do you want the programme to be (it is often valuable to agree at the end of one meeting the main topics likely to be considered at the following meeting while retaining the flexibility to switch in the light of changed circumstances)?

The role of the line manager

When you introduce coaching within your part of the organization do reflect on the role of the line manager, which in some cases will be you. A meeting between the coach and line manager is highly desirable at an early stage to establish a clear understanding of how an individual is perceived and what the expectations are for the future. Unless a coach knows the perspective of the client and the line manager the coach may lack the framework to take forward coaching effectively.

Involving the line manager could be in a one-to-one conversation between the coach and the line manager or in a three-way conversation
involving the client as well. The right approach will depend on the individual context as both arrangements can work very well. The key outcome
is the commitment of all three parties to work together to deliver desired
outcomes. The main values of the three-way conversation is to produce
a shared agenda and ensure any misconceptions are removed. The coach
ought to be pressing both parties when the coach senses there are differences of perception or priority which need to be worked on.

When you are not the direct line manager of somebody being coached
a more limited involvement would still be right. It could be encouraging
and participating in oral 360° feedback; it will certainly involve building a
shared perspective with the line manager about how an individual's senior
managers are going to contribute to the effectiveness of a coaching programme and how they are going to help the individual embed their own
learning from the coaching.

Ensuring successful outcomes

Coaching can become too cosy and comfortable, hence the importance of
clarity of outcomes. That does not mean that all the outcomes have to be
defined a year or six months in advance. Sometimes new issues arise where
outcomes can only be worked out at relatively short notice. Keeping a careful watch on whether coaching is having an impact while continuing to
maintain a distance so that the confidentiality of the coaching discussions
are absolute is part of proper management accountability. There will be
aspects of the coaching conversations that go wider than the original objectives, particularly when work and personal issues need to be interrelated
more effectively. There must be that element of trust that allows some of the
coaching time to be used on personal issues which need to be resolved so
that the individual's commitment at work is the more effective.

A good time to assess the effectiveness of coaching is when a renewal
point is reached. The main arguments for coaching beyond an initial period
are:

- to help continue to embed learning that has taken place in the initial
  period;
- to build on the challenging coaching relationship that has already been
  established which means that issues can often be dealt with quickly and
  efficiently;

- to stretch the boundaries further in terms of the individual's impact in their work;
- to extend further the learning from the first phase of coaching; and
- when the agenda has changed because the organization has changed radically or the individual has new responsibilities.

Roger had a leading role in a regional organization. He initially had six sessions of coaching and wanted to extend the coaching. He was clear that the benefits would be:

- taking forward the learning that had taken place during the first six months in a focused way;
- developing his personal impact with some key specified individuals;
- ensuring he made the best possible use of a national role to which he had just been appointed; and
- helping to ensure he developed effectively a set of organizational targets that are now part of his personal objectives.

When seeking agreement to a further phase of coaching Ric, a board member in a national organization, described how the previous phase had covered:

- working on his distinctive contribution as Finance Director in securing the organization's objectives;
- building key relationships with other partners to deliver the organization's objectives;
- management (and self-management) approach and style; and
- making an effective contribution at Board Meetings.

Looking ahead over the next phase he wanted to focus on:

- the delivery of immediate key outcomes (better closure of the annual accounts, efficiencies, a financial management review);
- developing further his board contribution;
- further work on getting right his style and impact with senior members of the organization; and
- next career steps.

It is often helpful to link a renewal of coaching with a commitment by an individual to changing direction or gear. This might be in response to the results of a performance review or to structural changes in the organization or the job. When someone wants to renew coaching it is perfectly reasonable for you to ask the following questions:

- How will the coaching help the individual to change gear in their role and respond to new requirements?
- How will the coaching help prepare somebody for future roles?
- Will the coaching be part of an effective cycle of renewal of energy?

If you are thinking of introducing a number of coaching assignments within your part of the organization it is crucial to meet with the Account Manager from the coaching organization you are thinking of using in order to build an understanding of the values of the coaching organization and the mix of skills of its coaches. It is worth building a picture of the range of approaches they take: be wary about any organization who sticks rigidly to one approach.

Piloting

Piloting can be an effective means of testing out what type of coaching is going to work within your organization and a means of assessing whether a particular coach or coaching organization is providing what you need. You might yourself act as the 'guinea pig' because of the potential benefits that your understanding of coaching will bring to introducing coaching effectively. Alternatively you might want to encourage a couple of volunteers. One of them might be addressing some specific issues while the other might be someone with potential to move higher up the organization.

Testing out a pilot with two or three people in different circumstances can produce a variety of evidence about what is helping make the coaching a success. Ideally the discussion of the results of the pilot are both with the individuals, their line managers and the coaches themselves in order to build a coherent perspective. But beware of the pilot that goes on for too long!

Taking forward a coaching culture

The development of coaching skills is not just for people who are professional coaches. An increasing number of line managers are themselves adopting coaching skills. Courses run by organizations like the School of Coaching provide line managers at senior levels with coaching skills. Developing coaching skills within your part of the organization could result from some individuals doing coaching courses, bringing in a qualified coaching trainer to do some workshops for your staff about coaching skills, or asking individuals who have been the beneficiaries of coaching to articulate how their learning has influenced the way they now lead and manage their staff.

Many organizations have been trying to embed a coaching style with senior leaders as firm champions. A good way of then embedding a coaching style is through the type of questions that are built into staff surveys. For example an organization that recently included in its staff survey the question, 'How good is your manager at adopting a coaching style?' produced a surge in requests for training in the development of coaching skills.

Persuading sceptics about coaching

To get the most out of coaching an individual has got to want to be present in the coaching conversation. It may take one or two meetings for somebody to move from sceptic to convert. A degree of scepticism at the start is helpful in ensuring that the coachee goes into the coaching sessions in a constructively critical way.

Some organizations have introduced coaching as a requirement. In our experience there will always be about 25% of the client group who start off sceptical and probably 5% to 10% who decide they are deriving no benefit after a couple of sessions. But the figures for those who decide they do not get value out of a compulsory participation in coaching are much lower than might be expected. Few people can resist the opportunity to talk about themselves in a focused one-to-one way. If the coach can then begin to help someone to piece together some of their attitudes and behaviour in a constructive way which has both personal and business benefits then scepticism can rapidly turn into delight.

Where pilots have gone well there will be advocates of coaching who will be the biggest influence on sceptical colleagues.

Evaluation

Because of the financial cost and opportunity cost of coaching, evaluation ought to be a key consideration. If coaching is being used for a wider area than your remit, evaluation that distinguishes the impact in different parts of the organization can be helpful. Satisfying yourself through asking key questions at the right moment can be just as effective as a large scale survey. Asking an individual to summarize how the coaching is benefiting them can reveal a great deal: it is not just the words they use but the extent to which there is a passion and an energy in the way they describe their learning from the coaching.

A key test for you might be whether the feedback that you are getting is that the coaching has been:

- **supportive:** enabling somebody to have a great level of self-awareness and develop a clearer set of priorities;
- **challenging:** in terms of developing ideas and perspectives; and
- **stretching:** enabling somebody to more effectively operate outside their comfort zone.

Conclusion

Good quality coaching will mean that individuals become more focused, assertive, self-aware and courageous. When coaching is used well the result will be a focused powerful impact. But if the organization is not ready for the energy that can come out of coaching, there can be an increased sense of frustration. Line managers need to be prepared to both encourage and respond to the impact of the coaching. Coaching should not be entered into 'lightly or wantonly' but in full awareness of the powerful effect it can have.

Chapter 13:

The International Dimension

Coaching can play a valuable role in addressing multicultural and international dimensions. This is going to become increasingly important. In this chapter, we look at five aspects of this engagement:

- at a one to one level where the differences in a person's culture and background are taken into account within the coaching session;
- at a wider macro level with an examination of coaching within black economic empowerment in post-apartheid South Africa;
- international consistency of standards of coaching;
- coaching managers and leaders of virtual teams; and
- making arrangements to put in place coaching across international boundaries.

A ll the way through this book we have worked on the assumption that leadership is a global phenomenon. It gets played out on a local, national and international stage. While many of our examples have expressed the international, even global dynamic, this chapter pulls together some specific international strands.

The fax, the telex and the telegram of twenty five years ago have given way to the video conference, the teleconference, the email and the text message. Now we have internet chat rooms, web blogs and instant communication via web cams attached to the computer and played through Messenger or Skype. The world is truly a global village with access to information instant and at times overwhelming.

There is still a crucial need to engage and communicate with people. Co-invention between coach and client gives renewed focus and energy. We summarized four key elements of engagement as 'future, themselves, business, family and community'. Coaches need to engage with clients in their community: no amount of modern technology and equipment can replace that process of engagement. This community will be increasingly global.

One-to-one coaching across cultural differences

Philippe Rosinski in his book *Coaching across Cultures* (2003) has expanded our notion of culture beyond that of nationality. There are corporate and professional cultures with which the coach will be working as well as the national cultural identity of the client. This makes for a rich mixture: there are many 'cultural' aspects for the coach to take into account – character and preference (e.g. using the Myers Briggs Preference Type Inventory which has been translated into several languages), and different types of background, beliefs and behaviours.

For coaching to be effective in this multi-cultural setting there are many guiding principles to be followed. In their excellent book *The CCL Handbook of Coaching* (2006), Lynne Delay and Maxine Dalton have highlighted fourteen principles in their chapter entitled 'Coaching across cultures' which we now comment upon in relation to our own experience:

1 *Build the relationship and take whatever time is needed*
   Many nationalities work on the principle that 'I have to get to know you, have a meal with you, before I can do business with you'. This is all part of the process of engagement and the same applies with coaching. The 'chemistry' meeting where the coach and client decide whether they can work with each other becomes especially important when the coach and client have different nationalities.
2 *Take more time with the assessment process*
   Assessing people in order to arrive at a working agenda for coaching, the coach will need to allow time to pick up nuances of language, ensure expectations are understood and to agree on the meaning behind the word 'development'.
3 *Don't rely on assumptions and ask when uncertain*
   Establishing the facts is a prerequisite in any coaching relationship especially in an international setting with which one is unfamiliar.
4 *Familiarize yourself with multiple cultural and leadership models*
   An early experience from Shell has stayed with Robin throughout his working life concerning the development of a Malaysian well-site by petroleum engineers for the oil industry. Local Sarawakian engineers were given government scholarships in the early 1980s to go to universities in the USA. A local Sarawakian who had grown up on a 'kampong aya' (village on the water) had attended university and by the

end of the second year had got to the point of challenging the lecturer (having been invited by the lecturer from day one to do so). He went home to his kampong and challenged the headman and found himself virtually thrown out of the village. What leadership model your client has in mind from their cultural background makes a big difference to the coaching.

5 *Learn the client's context, especially if he or she is working in a part of the organization or in a location that is less familiar to you*
Jane Upton coaches in Spain and is conscious of how some cultures are more open to coaching than others. One Spanish managing director commented to her that 'if a manager needs coaching then he shouldn't be in the job'. In the more traditional companies there is still a sense of assumed competence on appointment to senior roles and, in some cases, a fear of loss of face if 'development needs' are implied. In these situations, 'coaching as development' needs to be handled sensitively.

6 *Pay closer attention to your language, especially if you are coaching in English and your client's first language is not English*
Juan was a Marketing Manager for a medical supplies company in Spain. One of his challenges was to make his presence felt in international meetings; his level of English was good yet he found it difficult to react quickly enough during debates and was conscious of his language ability when compared to the native speakers in the room. Working on this at a slower and deliberate pace with his coach increased his perceived level and capability and certainly contributed to his promotion.

7 *Check frequently for understanding, especially if you are coaching in a language that is not the client's native tongue*
Jean was a Frenchman and was at a loss when confronted by the coach's phrase which 'slipped out' naturally during an exchange – 'So you are batting on a sticky wicket'!! This was meant to be an empathic commentary on Jean's getting bogged down in detail when under pressure, but the cricket analogy had no meaning for Jean.

8 *Learn to be comfortable with silence*
While this is an essential competence for a coach in any coaching relationship, it is particularly relevant in a cross cultural setting. It provides the client with the opportunity to think through their response.

9 *Develop ability to embrace a high degree of complexity and ambiguity*
Working with Matthieu, the managing director of a wholly owned research and development activity was complex. Understanding the 'power plays' within the organization was difficult enough, but Matthieu's French background and upbringing superimposed a totally different view of power and hierarchy. At the end of the coaching when Matthieu was asked what made him shift his behaviour, he said:

'The coach has to strike a chord and then the reaction is a shift. Your subconscious absorbs data. At some level you know you should be doing things differently. One day a coach holds a mirror up and makes you aware of the subconscious, helps put flesh on it and you can't avoid doing something about it – I am reminded of something which is evidently core to my interactions with people.'

10 *Do an honest appraisal of your cultural sensitivity and mental models*
There is no such thing as an objective question in coaching. A coach must always bring their subjective thinking/background/perception into the room and a question will always have a purpose. Self-awareness of the cultural perceptions is therefore even more critical in the international setting.

11 *Be coachable, and accept coaching from others, especially your client*
The opportunity to learn from the client who comes from outside your own culture is immense.

12 *Exercise a high degree of mental and behavioural resourcefulness*
The analogies, sporting metaphors and other 'illustrations' have to be thought through carefully. Use of a cricket analogy might work for those in Pakistan and India but will not work for those in France or Spain. Thinking into the client's situation and context requires a great deal of application and energy.

13 *Improve your global business knowledge*
The good executive coach who wants to work internationally will be as aware of the DAX and the NASDAQ as the FTSE 100 listings. International newswires and on line news via Reuters or the equivalent become essential. This is not just about global business but also about the global context in which business leadership development takes place. Decision makers need to take time out in an ever quicker change of business environment that changes ever quicker. In the University of Munster in Germany there is now a course on 'deceleration' to improve decision making or at least reduce risks!!

14 *Demonstrate high levels of empathy and respect for differences*
An awareness of the richness of diversity and differences between people is essential. A coach needs to be able to both see and feel that difference while working with it. An effective coach can work with all different nationalities if he looks at them as ingredients in this multicultural world to make not a 'soup' but a 'tossed salad', with every difference working together effectively while still being distinctive.

Coaching in the South African setting of black economic empowerment

As an example of how a number of these principles work out together in practice, we look briefly at coaching in South Africa where Ron Hyams is based as a coach. We start by describing the political and economic context for coaching.

Following the first full elections in South Africa in 1994 marking the end of the apartheid era, the country then faced the challenge of reversing the exclusion of black people from business. To this end South Africa introduced a framework of legislation, supported by voluntary industry charters.

Known as black economic empowerment (BEE) the goal initially was to increase levels of black ownership of South African business. Now, with 'broad based BEE' the approach extends to development, training and procurement. An agency called Empowerdex rates companies according to an empowerment index –and a good rating is now often an entry ticket to gaining business, particularly in the government sector.

BEE's impact has been to help to increase the representation of black executives as owners and managers of South African business. The favourable socio-economic and political climate and the growing middle class have lead to a consumer lead boom – with growth rates approaching 6%. The result is a skills shortage and the need to develop black leaders, particularly at the top of industry, plus a need to create much more employment further down.

Getting more black South Africans into the board rooms of industry is not just a numbers issue. The challenge is to create a whole culture change – requiring new attitudes and eliminating bias at all levels – changed recruitment, selection, development, retention and remuneration. Only in this way will more black managers come into and through the development pipeline – but all this takes time.

Coaching has huge potential to accelerate the progress of black talent up the experience curve. In this section Ron Hyams, founder of the South African office of Praesta describes a series of case studies to provide a snapshot of some of the cultural challenges of coaching in South Africa. He also describes how coaching can contribute to leadership development – for both black and white individuals – particularly at the upper end of South African industry.

Our first case study describes a situation where Ron Hyams was brought in to coach a PepsiCo International Marketing Director, a company which is progressive in its people management policies and gives equal weight to the achievement of business and people objectives. The challenge is to quantify the people objectives. The client's 360° feedback scores were impressive. However, she was not satisfied with this level of data and asked Ron if he could explore further. Ron met with her direct reports face-to-face to focus in on the behaviours that would make a difference to her effectiveness as a leader. Face-to-face meetings can help people articulate their ideas about what they want to say to their manager.

Ron interviewed her various reports and colleagues including one of the Simba R & D directors, Fru Nche, who is African and whose feedback was about a seemingly innocuous piece of behaviour: she tended to keep her phone on during meetings or when walking down the corridors. The result was that she sometimes seemed less than fully present.

Fru commented:

> 'In most African cultures more junior people prefer a senior person to look them in the face, nod, and acknowledge them. Otherwise there can be misunderstanding. In a way the challenges in South Africa are not special – every organization in every country has to deal with dif-ference – of function, of personality and of seniority. However, here the black/white dynamic cannot be ignored. For many African people English is not their first language so when they speak to their white col-leagues their accent is not "right" and they find it hard to express them-selves – that can un-nerve them. A cycle can develop where they are perceived as lacking in confidence and that in turn makes it even harder to get their message across. So the white person's doubts about them can become self-fulfilling. Their white colleague may not be thinking in terms of colour – and yet, if they don't understand the cultural context there can be misunderstanding. They may just want people who can perform – that sounds fine in theory – but there has to be sensitivity to the cultural nuances that influence behaviour. In my culture there's always a hierarchy towards the elder who is due respect because of age, experience or seniority. A senior director is held in high respect and they, in turn, need to honour this by showing that they are listening. Otherwise the cycle of respect given and respect received breaks down and trust and performance can suffer.'

Ron encouraged the client to meet with the colleagues who had given her feedback so that she could fully understand their point of view. Through this process she became much more aware of the impact of her distracted listening.

This motivated her to work with Ron on a programme of change. The actions included switching off her phone in meetings and set up a weekly rota to talk to more junior people on the factory floor. When Ron spoke to

Fru some months later he commented that the changes in the client's be-haviour as a result of coaching had definitely increased her credibility and respect as a leader.

BEE was initially focused on increasing black ownership of business. Now with 'broad based black empowerment' the criteria are more wide ranging and encompass criteria such as procurement from black suppliers and provision for black training and development.

To this extent achieving transformation is more than a 'nice to have': rather it is a pressing commercial imperative particularly for companies seeking to do business with the government sector. This is the context for our next case study – the coaching of Collin, a talented young 'high po-tential' at T-Systems, one of South Africa's top IT Company. The coaching was not just about transformation or empowerment. Rather it was about doubling the turnover of a particular part of the business and winning new government contracts. However, the company also recognized the irresist-ible business case for increasing the representation of people of colour on their senior management team. Much of their business is with parastatals and to win government work they knew that they had to improve their BEE profile.

Collin was very committed to BEE because of his own personal history and the early experience of seeing his father arrested and jailed for a night for being found on the 'wrong side' (the white side) of the beach which gave him a hunger to succeed and prove himself. Through coaching Col-lin worked through his own limiting mindsets and fear that he would not win true respect from his colleagues; the concern being they'd say 'he's too young – just a BEE appointment'. Collin was a voracious learner, and used the coaching to rapidly become a wise and confident leader. His early fears evaporated as he saw himself grow in stature and confidence. His boss com-mented, 'He's been in the leadership team for a few months – but it's as if he's been here for years.' Collin was targeted by head hunters and offered big incentives to leave. However, he had the maturity to see that he needed to stay with his current employer to build a solid foundation of skills.

In reality very little of the work with Collin was about racial differences. The focus was often more on differences of thinking style than differences of cultural style. Myers Briggs was used to help Collin understand his own style (big picture, not very keen on the detail) and how this impacted on others. Coaching worked well for Collin. One of his colleagues commented: 'I've seen him grow from someone proving themselves as a leader to some-one who is a capable and confident leader'. As Collin put it, 'you've given me the mandate to be confident, to have unquestionable faith in myself – coaching has enabled me to access more of my own wisdom'.

South Africa, the Rainbow nation, has a rich tapestry of cultures. Its challenge is to throw off the legacy of apartheid and develop economically to create jobs and heal what is still a divided society. Coaching has a key role in terms of empowering people and accelerating the movement of historically disadvantaged individuals up the experience curve. Coaches have to be aware of the complex and multi-layered cultural context. They also have to remember that generalizations about culture are just guides and avoid the danger of stereotyping. Each client is a unique individual – and the coach has to let go all cultural assumptions – and find out what is the particular client's story, challenge and dream.

International consistency of standards

Coaching is a young and emerging profession. There is no single body which acts as the professional body for all coaches. It is not surprising, therefore, for there to be an increasing clamour by organisations for coaches to provide evidence of their coaching credentials.

Many universities from Australia to America offer postgraduate courses in coaching. The American based International Coach Federation (ICF) has members worldwide and as recently as 2006 has instituted a suite of professional standards from basic to master in order to help coaches 'benchmark' themselves. The World Association of Business Coaches (WABC) based in Canada is developing a worldwide set of standards to enable business coaches to position themselves with clients and sponsors in their coaching markets. The European Mentoring and Coaching Council (EMCC) has instituted a set of quality standards from Foundation to Masters which enables coaching training organizations, universities and coaching practices to 'benchmark' themselves.

The scene of developing standards is emergent. It is hoped that the various bodies, of which ICF, WABC and EMCC are but three, will come together and coordinate their various sets of standards. It is certain that if the 'profession' of coaching doesn't regulate itself sensibly then the various governments and governmental bodies (European Union not being the least) will do so on their behalf. Further details of these three bodies are available on their websites: www.wabccoaches.com, www.coachfederation.org and www.emccouncil.org.

Coaching managers and leaders of virtual teams

In the global marketplace, services, goods and people are traded globally. Leaders find themselves managing teams of individuals dispersed over many locations. Face to face team meetings are held bi-monthly or quarterly at best, otherwise all the contact is by phone, email or video link.

These virtual international teams generate their own pressures and tensions for senior executives. A coach of anyone in this situation will find themselves having either nil or minimal face to face contact with the client. We highlight four key areas for the coach to ensure they remain effective. Any organization who engages a coach to work internationally needs to be satisfied that the coach can handle these aspects:

1   *Business and client's culture*
    A coach working in the English language and with a client whose native language is not English faces at least two distinct challenges. What is the client's own cultural background and what has made them the leader they are? What is the international business culture of the organization within which the client is working?

    Trevor Childs coaches in Belgium and has been working with a group of oil and gas company senior executives. The three senior executives are of different nationalities and are working on a shared focused agenda of development. Trevor received an extensive briefing of the global business strategy of the organization, rendered more anecdotal by the three executives. In order to understand the setting of one of the executives, Trevor spent two days 'shadowing' him with some members of his team in Singapore and was able to provide on the spot feedback on what they had agreed to explore as development objectives. Getting an actual physical experience of the client in his team setting enabled the coaching to become more alive and effective.

2   *Get used to telephone coaching and a long day*
    Robin is working with a managing director of a law firm based in Hong Kong. The 'head office' of the firm is based in the Americas and the managing partner works in and with two teams – his bosses and peers in the Americas (who seek to have direct input to his local firm marketing strategy) and his team in Hong Kong of local partners (who seek to have their own priorities in marketing locally).

    The coaching is being undertaken by teleconference as well as occasionally by video conference. There are issues of time difference, misinterpretations of colleagues email messages and correspondence ('why don't they understand the problems we have locally?') and conflicting priorities of global and local strategies especially affecting profitability. Working through these issues while taking account of local and global pressures and cultures is demanding for the coach as well as the managing partner.

3 *Put yourself out to meet face-to-face*

Chris was an executive in the Operations part of an investment bank. In charge of 1000 people worldwide he was also part of an organization which was 'New York centric' and thus had many peers and reports as well as his overall Executive team boss in America and around the world. Chris's coach had to ensure that whenever the boss was in the UK, the coach could have access to him. This was especially important at the beginning of the coaching relationship so that the boss could provide his input to the development agenda and its business context. The coach recollected a focused hour's meeting in a hotel in London before the boss went into a corporate dinner and after his plane had been delayed. The information obtained, the nuances explained and the interpretation accorded to Chris's development agenda provided an essential start to the coaching.

4 *All-round reviews*

The value of 360° feedback is rapidly becoming a requirement as an input to coaching and development. In the international context we find that there is a descending order of effectiveness in the way the 360° reviews are undertaken because of cultural differences:

- most effective – face-to-face interviews with peers, bosses and subordinates when visiting, e.g. the head office in Paris, when the client is based in London.
- reasonably effective – combination of face-to-face and telephone interviews. In a banking culture, e.g. a trading floor the phone is a highly acceptable and common medium. It is less common a medium in industrial and commercial companies but if used sensitively and the process is set up by the client through a personal introduction by the client of the coach for those taking part, then it is effective.
- less effective – when questions are put in writing over email or a computer based questionnaire and there is no validation, interpretation or elucidation and questioning of the written word.

Making arrangements for international coaching

As organizations are increasingly global there is both an increased need for coaching in order to enable individuals to take account of cultural differences and a need for consistency in coaching standards. Good quality coaching must take account of international reach and the balancing of local circumstances and global imperatives.

Working with a coaching organization with partners across the globe enables a consistency of values and a common understanding about desired outcomes.

Where coaching is required to be provided by one or more suppliers for its executive cadre worldwide, an organization needs to pay especial attention to the following checklist of some key questions to be asked of that supplier:

1 In which locations can the coaching firm provide coaches?
2 Can the coaches coach in the local language and a shared international language such as English?
3 What personal experience do the coaches have of working internationally?
4 What experience do the coaches have in coaching cross-culturally?
5 What other clients of the coaching firm have requested and been provided with this international service?
6 What is the organisation's coaching philosophy and approach?
7 Will the proposed coaches agree to be interviewed for suitability?
8 Will the coaches work with the organization's competency framework?
9 Will the organization provide an up-date of whether or not meetings have taken place?
10 Will the coaching firm submit to satisfaction surveys and on going measurement/evaluation of coaching?
11 How does the coaching firm ensure consistent coaching standards worldwide?
12 Are all coaches supervised independently and regularly?
13 How will the line manager of the coaching client be feeding into the coaching based in a different country?
14 How will the coaching firm ensure a good match between coach and client?
15 What use will be made of telephone coaching, webcam or video conferencing if the need arises?
16 What value-added is provided by the coaching firm to the client?

The arrangements put in place by PepsiCo in managing its international coaching requirements address these questions.The following is based on personal conversations with David Oliver who is the Director of Organization and Management Development (OMD) for PepsiCo International (all operations outside the US and Canada) based in New York. He organizes coaching for a potential of 1000 executives internationally. The current focused programme has between 60 and 75 coaching assignments at the top level. Since PepsiCo operates in 200 countries, this represents a truly global challenge.

Salient features of the PepsiCo process are:

- Coaching is provided for those identified with general manager potential or potential as a senior functional leader. It is not for those 'in difficulty'. It is a business investment;
- It is tied into succession or 'People Planning' as PepsiCo call it. Coaching is also provided for those identified as future senior leaders via the International Leadership Development Programme;
- All coaches go through an application screening process and some are then invited to attend the Certification Programme held in New York over a couple of days. David and others take people through the tools used by PepsiCo (e.g. psychometrics, assessment and others) as well as the process and approach to talent management;
- All coaches together with local HR people from PepsiCo around the world look at a case study of a 'real person with real data' which is anonymized;
- Coaches are asked to provide their insights and also the approaches and tactics they might adopt with the client in the case study as they coach.
- David and the other HR people assess what they observe and undertake both a cultural (to PepsiCo) and competence 'fit'. The key questions are:
  - 'Would we be comfortable with the person going in front of a high potential?'
  - As important as the question above, 'Will the coach enhance the person's development for future PepsiCo roles?' or Will the coach add value to the person's development experience?'
- Local HR people can best fit the coach (whom they have observed) to the high potential client as they seek to 'match'. The intention always is to have a centralized process but provide local autonomy in the matching.

What are David's biggest challenges?

> 'There aren't enough hours in my day! Managing a global network is just one of my many responsibilities. Time is spent interacting with the coaches and local HR, getting status updates, providing access to materials (e.g. assessments, PepsiCo tools) and providing updates to senior management.
>
> 'Making connections between coaches and between coaches and clients is the biggest challenge. We use teleconferencing, email and communicate through the local HR people (who really own and

manage the day-to-day). We ensure status updates in each of four phases of coaching and receive on-line progress reports from coaches in each assignment.

'*We feel the certification program gives us a crucial opportunity to connect with coaches, teach them about our company and our approach and give us a chance to evaluate them. Even though coaches were pre-screened before attending the certification program, there were some coaches we chose not to use because the coach was not right for our organization. Finding that out during the certification stage is much better than after pairing a coach with an executive and having a bad experience.*

'*What we need are coaches who are locally relevant and understand the local culture and who also can be focused on the broader agenda for PepsiCo. A coach who understands China and in particular the local culture but who cannot understand interactions with PepsiCo Head Office is no good for us. We need coaches to service both dimensions.*'

Conclusion

In this chapter we have sought to explore the multicultural issues facing coaching before it can be deemed effective in an international setting. Executives are changing jobs and moving about the world in ever increasing numbers. As coaches will be working with many different nationalities it will be vital that they not only adopt the guiding principles set out earlier in the chapter, but also adapt their means of engagement with their clients and be adept at demonstrating their credentials.

Chapter 14:

Engaging with the Future of Coaching

This chapter offers reflections on the future of coaching. It does not provide a precise definition of what coaching will look like in ten years' time, but there are clear trends. The chapter addresses:

- changing business needs;
- development in good coaching practice;
- the impact of technology;
- professional underpinning; and
- greater emphasis on whole-of-life coaching.

It suggests that the future success of coaching depends on the ability to ensure freshness and vitality in coaching conversations, approaches and outcomes. The future of coaching depends on a cadre of coaches able to engage, challenge and stretch, so that the leaders they work with consistently 'play at the top of their game'.

Our belief is that coaching is going to grow as a profession. As the world goes faster and faster, more than ever individuals are going to need the opportunity to take time out to reflect with a 'trusted other'. The trusted other may be a spouse, partner, friend, companion, work colleague, mentor, advisor or internal or external coach. Within that matrix of personal support, the independent coach has a distinctive contribution to make.

All these individuals can encourage and support, but often the coach is in the best possible position to stretch and challenge. The coach sees an individual through independent eyes. Theirs are not rose-tinted glasses: they bring an objectivity and a rigour that can both support and stretch, and can both bring companionship and challenge. If coaching is primarily about enabling an individual to address their work and the whole of their life in a focused, purposeful and more holistic way, then the need for this resource is likely to get stronger and not weaker.

Changing business needs

Changing business needs where coaching has a major contribution are:

- organizations operating faster and faster;
- addressing global changes and opportunities;
- the changing shape of leadership;
- the need for clarity of results at each stage;
- making the most of multicultural diversity;
- re-skilling people on a regular cycle, or enabling them to move on to new spheres;
- ever increasing focus on innovation; and
- a growing emphasis on values and social responsibility.

These changing business needs have a clear impact on coaching requirements.

- **Organizations operating faster and faster**: the evermore rapid speed of communication means that decisions are required instantly. There is a pressure to be infinitely adaptable. Coaching can enable somebody to make sense of change that is operating at incessant speed. It provides a space to think, and to reflect on different options. Without that opportunity to stand back, 'faster and faster' can become a spiral with no purpose.
- **Addressing global changes and opportunities**: coaches operating at senior levels need to bring an international understanding or be part of an international network. If an individual is moving from job to job globally, there needs to be a consistency in the quality of coaching support. Coaches must be able to relish the international dimension and enable an individual to develop the capacity to work effectively in a global world.
- **The changing shape of leadership**: leadership is becoming increasingly networked within and across organizations. Companies are becoming vertically and horizontally integrated. What were competitor organizations for ABC plc are now part and parcel of the delivery mechanisms of ABC. Leaders need to operate across this and network themselves in different ways. Coaching can help to make these connections. Getting the best out of people and getting them to give a significant part of their

discretionary energy to the organization is becoming increasingly complicated.

- **The need for clarity of results**: the drive to deliver becomes ever stronger with evidence of relative performance often being immediately available. Hence the need for coaching based on clear objectives and desired outcomes: unless coaching can demonstrate that it is enabling somebody to deliver their outcomes, it will become an expensive luxury rather than an essential tool. It is perfectly possible to combine a focus on results in coaching with the opportunity for open-ended discussion on issues that are important to the individual. But coaching must never be allowed to drift off into the self-indulgent. The delivery of results has to be paramount. John Charlton, editor of *Training and Coaching Magazine*, is clear that 'one thing that matters to purchasers of coaching is that coaches provide them with a coherent approach that includes, within its scope, measurable outcomes. This helps those who procure coaching to demonstrate that it can provide a definable return on investment, something that is becoming increasingly *de rigeur* for many HR and training directors'.

- **Making the most of multicultural diversity**: any nation or city needs to embrace the wealth of cultures within it. Overcoming prejudice and rigid perspectives is crucial to both economic and social success. Good coaching can enable individuals to appreciate multicultural diversity. At the centre of the work we did on the Pathways Programme for high-potential members of ethnic minorities within UK government departments were the twin objectives of enabling individuals to draw positively from their cultural background and at the same time developing their confidence in dealing with new and very different situations.

- **Enabling people to go through continuous learning and to move on**: coaching focused on an individual can help ensure effective learning and then give somebody the confidence to move on to new spheres. In his book *Finding your Future: the second time around*, Peter explores how best to take stock and then move on, looking at themes like learning through failure, coping with fears, following fascinations, moving on from frustrations, deciding on fundamentals and crystallizing what is most important about personal fulfilment. Coaching can provide a means of inter-relating different frustrations and fascinations, and so can help an individual work through to a coherent set of next steps.

- **Ever increasing focus on innovation**: organizations that are successful will have a strong emphasis on continuous innovation. The pace of technological change and the expectations of customers mean that the organization that does not innovate will die. Effective coaching will enable key individuals to keep fresh and alert and to push the boundaries of their thinking. A coach encouraging an individual to stretch their creativity further and go beyond previous boundaries is going to be so important for success.

- **A growing emphasis on values and social responsibility**: many organizations will try to differentiate themselves by defining their values in a way which motivates and engages their staff. Linked to this is likely to be an increased focus on social responsibility, starting with looking at energy and environmental decisions. Where coaching is focused on enabling somebody to integrate organizational and personal values, it can reinforce both. If an organization is focusing on social responsibility issues, then coaching can help ensure that corporate and personal responsibility are aligned. It can enable learning from voluntary activities to be drawn back into an individual's competence and development in the organizational world.

Developments in coaching good practice

Some of the factors influencing the development over the next few years in coaching good practice include:

- it is now increasingly acceptable for a senior leader to have a coach;
- coaching is less something that is done behind closed doors and is now an accepted part of the development of a leader; and
- there is a growing acceptance that effective coaching brings together a sound psychological understanding and personal experience of leadership.

Without direct leadership experience a coach's perspective is bound to be one-sided.

Some of the key developments likely to happen over the next few years are laid below.

- **An increased focus on real-time coaching of individuals**: i.e. a client being content for a coach to spend a day observing them, talking to those who work with them and feeding back observations. The most powerful of coaching sessions can come at the end of a day that has been rich in variety and where the coach has seen an individual in a wide range of different settings.
- **Real time coaching with teams**: i.e. where a coach has been observing a team and then asking pertinent questions and feeding back reflec-

tions. Enabling a team to assess objectively how it is working and then move on can enable it to cope with the pace of change in a positive and harmonious way, minimizing the risk of self-destruction.

- **Coaching is likely to become more integrated into business development programmes and business school courses**: the best of courses always acknowledge that embedding the learning is crucial – coaching discussions at crucial moments can enable somebody to reflect on that learning and ensure the benefits are not lost.

- **The greater use of a structured mentoring relationship for a client alongside an external coach**: this already happens in the best of programmes. Further developing the complementary impact of mentor and coach is going to be an effective way of maximizing the benefit of financial investment. With challenge from two complementary sources, an individual will find it more difficult to hide from necessary action.

- **The development of the role and contribution of the leadership development expert within an organization**: an increasing number of organizations are creating a role where a central person builds up an understanding of the needs of individuals and the capacity of coaching to help. The advice given to a coach from this central expert can be invaluable in setting the right direction and perspective for the coaching. It can help maximize the benefits for the employing organization.

- **A clearer relationship between building emotional awareness in people and the delivery of results**: it is essential that the individual client develops clear emotional self-awareness. Even at a basic level, an individual's profile can lead to a better understanding of the relationship between an individual's personality and the best way of encouraging or stimulating them to reach desired results. There will be a growing number of psychometric tools; it is important that they are used sensitively and not in a blanket or rigid way.

- **Coaching becoming part of an individual's contractual relationship**: an individual executive's job changes are becoming more frequent and varied as their career develops. The ingredients in the leadership agenda change regularly. As a result, what was seen to be an arrangement for a specific purpose for coaching at a point in time now becomes an ongoing relationship. A motor vehicle has an annual MOT to check fitness for purpose. In the same way executives will seek to build coaching into their contractual relationships with organizations, to ensure their own 'fitness for purpose'.

- **Developing and reinforcing a coaching culture in an organization**: the individual who treasures the time spent with a coach will instinctively want to create similar situations for their staff which might be encouraging them to have with their own coach. Creating an organization in which there is a culture of coaching can provide the increased levels of confidence and risk taking that will enable an organization to move on more quickly than it might otherwise have done.

- **Building partnerships between individuals both internally within an organization and externally**: the bigger an organization the more its reputation depends on the quality of the myriad of interactions between people within the organization and with key partners. Keeping those partnerships healthy based on trust and a shared sense of direction is essential for any organization to survive. Coaching which focuses on ensuring quality in relationships will be increasingly important in embedding a sense of flow and dynamism in any organization.
- **The use of specific coaching skills for different purposes**: top sportsmen may have different coaches for different skills. The ubiquitous coach who gets to know an individual well is likely to be the norm but, for somebody in a very demanding position, coaching conversations with different people will enable them to develop different aspects of their performance. A range of skill needs might include; giving presentations, building partnerships, personal impact, developing a strategy for the future or ensuring personal wellbeing. We will often suggest that a client meets with a different coach to work through particular issues. This flexibility within one coaching organization is going to become increasingly important in the future.
- **The use of short-focused interventions**: these would be less about building a relationship between coach and client and more about addressing some very sharply defined issues.

The impact of technology

Technology will have an ever increasing impact on coaching. Relevant factors are:

- the immediacy with which information is available on the Internet about organizations, ideas and individuals;
- the speed with which different people can be consulted;
- the devastating effect that information overload can have on the wellbeing of individuals and their capacity to make decisions; and
- the increased flexibility of communication between coach and client.

The heart of coaching work will continue to be face-to-face discussion. But once two individuals know each other, telephone coaching is perfectly feasible. Telephone coaching across continents will become increasingly common as a coach builds up understanding of a particular global business.

As the webcam becomes more available this will enable coaching conversations to take account of the visual as well as the audio signals. The impact of the introduction of webcam should not be overestimated as telephone coaching can work perfectively effectively. But for many people seeing the coach visually at the same time as hearing them can help ensure the experience is effective and without too much distraction. It is sometimes too easy to be talking with somebody on the telephone and still looking at the emails. With the webcam picture it would be too embarrassing to show this indulgence!

Coaching through email has grown in its use. Where it is part of a face-to-face coaching relationship it is a valuable adjunct. But we are sceptical about whether on its own purely email contact provides enough depth of relationship for coaching to have its fullest impact.

What is clear is that coaching must take very careful account of developments in technology. Coaches must try to embrace the technologies that their (invariably younger!) clients use as a matter of course. They must respond to those changes and not be Luddites. At the same time it is the quality of human interaction between coach and coachee that will ensure the success of coaching and not the speed of exchange through information technology. The trend to more bespoke individual approaches to coaching is perhaps a push back to the increasing use of technology in daily life.

Professional underpinning

The coaching profession is not very clearly defined or regulated. Because it has grown up from two different strands (i.e. occupational psychologists and those with business leadership experience) there has been a lack of coherence. Inevitably debates about the profession start from either the importance of the occupational psychology background, or the necessity of a business background. Our perspective is that experience of business leadership and awareness of psychological underpinnings are both crucial. Developments over the next few years are likely to include the following.

- Development in the quality and effectiveness of supervision: this can currently be a bit random but is likely to become more structured.
- The oversight of the profession through a professional body covering standards, competence, quality, supervision and CPD: this is likely to happen but there is a tension about the principles on which it will be based.

- Further development of psychological underpinnings: the continued focus on emotional awareness is likely to lead to ever more useful instruments which can then provide a perspective on an individual's psychological make up and preferences.
- Increased use of 360° feedback: this would cover a wider cross-section of people from different stakeholders and non-work environments.

Greater emphasis on the whole of life coaching

Our belief is that coaching will increasingly focus on the whole of life covering some of the following issues:

- **Transitions between different phases of life**: this is not just between different jobs but is addressing how different experiences lead into a new set of aspirations for the next phase of life. It is about encouraging individuals to view positively each of their life experiences so that the next phase builds effectively on the previous one even though the individual may be going in a rather different direction.
- **Coaching involving an individual's partner as well as the individual**: we are increasingly finding a pattern whereby an individual will ask the coach to have a conversation with the spouse or partner. We walk into this territory carefully but often understanding issues that are important in a home environment feeds straight back into understanding how somebody is prioritising their energy at work. Where an individual wants to change their behaviour, a coalition between coach and partner can be an effective alliance of support. As the working world moves faster and faster the need for an individual to have both a peaceful family life and an active life with their children becomes all the more important.
- **The focus on the holistic growth of an individual covering physical, intellectual, economic, emotional and spiritual well-being**: no one part of life can be seen in isolation. The well-being or frustration in one aspect of life will rapidly flow into other areas. We are convinced that all these five areas are important and mutually interdependent. The future of coaching needs to recognize this interdependence.

Freshness

The future of any coaching relationship depends on ensuring freshness and vitality in coaching conversations, approaches and outcomes. This is just as true at the individual level as in the relationship between a coaching organization and a directorate or employing organization. Staleness is the blight that kills coaching. The coach must keep fresh in terms of energy, ideas and approaches. The coaching organization must be alert, responsive and dynamic. Coaching conversations must always be engaging, encouraging and demanding.

Coaching, if it is to continue to be in the ascendant, must keep that unique quality of engagement where the individual feels both enlivened and at peace with themselves, stretched but not squashed and enabled but not exhausted. The future of coaching depends on a cadre of coaches who can find the right wavelength to enable somebody to bring together the purposes that matter most to them and grow into the person they aspire to be.

Annex 1:

Introducing Coaching Programmes: Key Questions

The considerations when introducing coaching will vary from organization to organization. The following list of 21 key questions can provide a good starting point for reflecting on the context, choices about the coaching and the implementation and evaluation of the coaching.

Context

1 What outcomes do you need to deliver as an organization?
2 What type of organization do you want to become? What is your vision?
3 What are the values that you want to drive the organization?
4 Where do you want senior leaders to bring most value-added?
5 How do you want to maintain vitality in the organization?
6 What are the development needs that are most important across the organization?
7 What are the key external factors you need to prepare people for?

Coaching choices

8 Where do you see coaching helping to meet the development needs?
9 What coaching outcomes do you particularly want to see?
10 What type of coaching organization or organizations are you wanting to work with?
11 What is the balance between senior business experience and an understanding of psychological perspectives in the coaching work?

12 Is there experience of coaching within the organization you can build on?

13 How might you encourage 'buy in' to the benefits of coaching?

14 What sort of selection procedure might you adopt for choosing a coach?

Coaching implementation

15 How much time is your organization willing to set aside for the briefing of coaches?

16 How do you want to position one-to-one coaching alongside team development or learning sets?

17 How precise do you want the objectives for each individual to be for the coaching?

18 To what extent do you want oral 360° feedback to be part of the input to the coaching?

19 How much involvement of the line manager should there be in discussions with the coach?

20 What sort of generic feedback about overall themes are you looking for if a number of people are being coached?

21 How will you evaluate the coaching?

Annex 2:

Bibliography

Adair, J. (2005), *How to Grow Leaders*, London: Kogan Page

Adair, J. (1988), *Action Centred Leadership*, London: Kogan Page

Allan, J., Kingdom, M., Murrin, K. and Rudkin, D. (1999),*?What If!:How to Start a Creative Revolution at Work*, Chichester: Capstone

Badaracco, J. (2002), *Leading Quietly: An Unorthodox Guide to Doing the Right Thing*, Harvard: Harvard Business School

Bennis, W. and Goldsmith, J. (2003), *Learning to Lead*, Cambridge, MA: Perseus

Borg, J. (2004), Persuasion: *The Art of Influencing People*, Harlow: Pearson

Boyatziv, R. and McKee A. (2005), *Resonant Leadership*, Boston, Massachusetts: Harvard Business School

Bridges, W. (1980), *Transitions Making Sense of Life's Changes*, Cambridge, MA: Perseus

Brearley, M. (1985), *The Art of Captaincy*, London: Hodder and Stoughton

Bryce, L. (2002), *The Coach*, London: Piatkus

Bunyan, J. (1943), *Pilgrim's Progress*, London: Collins

Cameron, E. and Green M. (2004), *Making Sense of Change Management*, London: Kogan

Center for Creative Leadership (2004), *Handbook of Leadership Development*, San Francisco: Jossey-Bass

Chapman, T., Best, B. and Van Casteren (2003), *Executive Coaching: Exploding the Myths*, Basingstoke: Palgrave

Chartered Institute of Personal and Development, (2007), *Coaching Supervision: Maximising the Potential of Coaching*, London: CIPD

Coffee, E. (2002), *10 Things that Keep CEOs Awake*, London: McGraw-Hill

Collins, J. (2001), *Good to Great*, New York: Harper

Clutterbuck, D. and Megginson, D. (2005), *Making Coaching Work*, London: CIPD

Curtis, M. (1981), *Great Political Theories (Volume 1)*, New York: Avon

Dagley, G. (2006), *Human Resource Professionals' Perceptions of Executive Coaching, Vol 1, Issue No.2*, International Coaching Psychology Review: The British Psychological Society

Day, D. (2001), *Leadership Development – A Review in Context*, Article published in Leadership Quarterly ll(4)

Delay, L. and Dalton, M. (2006), '*Coaching Across Cultures*' in the CCL Handbook of Coaching ed. S. Ting and P. Seisco, San Francisco: Jossey-Bass

Downey, M. (2003), *Effective Coaching*, London: Texere (Thomson)

Drath, W. (2001), *The Deep Blue Sea*, San Francisco: Jossey-Bass

Egan, GT. (2002), *The Skilled Helper*, Pacific Grove USA: Brooks/Cole

Elsner, R. and Farrands, B. (2006), *Lost in Transition*, Marshall Cavendish

Goffee, R. and Jones, G. (2006), *Why Should Anyone be Lead by You?*, Boston, Massachusetts: Harvard Business School

Goldratt, E. and Cox, J. (1993), *The Goal*, England: Gower

Goleman, D. (2002), *The New Leaders*, London: Little Brown

Goleman, D. (2006), *Social Intelligence*, London: Hutchinson

Greenleaf, R.K. (1996), *On Becoming a Servant Leader*, San Francisco: Jossey-Bass

Hardingham, A. (2006), '*The British Eclectic Model in Practice*', Article from the International Journal of Mentoring and Coaching Volume IV, Issue 1, February 2006

Haskins, N. (2005), *A Qualitative Inquiry into Leadership Development in a Law Firm*, Unpublished Masters dissertation, School of Management, University of Surrey

Hawkins, P. and Smith, N. (2006), *Coaching, mentoring and organisational consultancy: supervision and development*, Milton Keynes: Open University Press

Hersey, Dr P. (1985), *The Situational Leader*, USA: Warner Books

Hofstede, Prof. G. (2004), *Cultures and Organisations*, London: McGraw-Hill

Hudson, F.M. (1999), *The Handbook of Coaching*, New York: Jossey-Bass

Jaworski, J. (1996), *Synchronicity*, San Francisco: Berrett-Koehler

Kay, D. and Hinds, R. (2002), *A Practical Guide to Mentoring*, Oxford: How to Books Ltd

Kegan, R. (2006), *The Evolving Self*, USA: Harvard University Press

Kotter, J.P. (1995), *Leading Change: Why Transformation Efforts Fail*, Harvard: Harvard Business Review

Lee, G. (2003), *Leadership Coaching*, London: CIPD

Lencioni, P. (2002), *The Five Dysfunctions of a Team*, San Francisco: Jossey-Bass

Mant, A. (1997), *Intelligent Leadership*, Australia: Allen and Unwin

McDermott, I. and Jago, W.C. (2003), *The NLP Coach*, London: Piatkus

McGovern, J., Vergara, M., Murphy, S., Barker, L. and Warrenfeltz, R. (2001), *Maximising the impact of Exectuvie Coaching*, The Manchester Review, Vol. 6, Number 1

Mind Gym, The (2005), *The Mind Gym: Wake your Mind up*, London: Time Warner

Moss Kanter, R. (1990), *When Giants Learn to Dance*, London: Unwin Hyman

O'Neil, J. (1993), *The Paradox of Success*, England: McGraw-Hill

Owen, H. (2000), *In Search of Leaders*, Chichester, London: Nicholas Brealey

Permick, R. (2001), *Creating a Leadership Development Programme – 9 Essential Tasks*, Article published in Public Personnel Management 30(4)

Rosinski, P. (2003), *Coaching Across Cultures*, London: Nicholas Brealey

Shaw, P. A. (2005), *Conversation Matters: How to Engage Effectively with One Another*, London: Continuum

Shaw, P.A. (2006), *Finding Your Future: A Second Time Around*, London: Darton, Longman and Todd

Shaw, P. A. (2006), *The 4 Vs of Leadership: Vision, Values, Value-Added and Vitality*, Chichester: Capstone

Thompson, P., Graham, J. and Lloyd, T. (2005), *A Woman's Place is in the Boardroom*, Basingstoke: Palgrave Macmillan

Thier, M.J. (2003), *Coaching Clues*, London: Nicholas Brealey

Watkins, M. *The First 90 Days*, Boston, Massachusetts: Harvard Business School Press

West, L. and Milan, M. (2001), *The Reflecting Glass*, Basingstoke: Palgrave

Whitmore, J. (1992), *Coaching for Performance*, London: Nicholas Brealey

Zeus, P. and Skiffington, S. (2002), *The Coaching at Work Toolkit*, Roseville Australia: McGraw Hill

Index